P9-BIC-180

The Alps I Love

the ALPS I love...

Introduction by
MAURICE HERZOG

Titles by
MAX ALDEBERT

Text by
GUILLAUME HANOTEAU

Photographs by
MICHAEL SERRAILLIER

TUDOR PUBLISHING COMPANY
NEW YORK

DEPARTURE at three a.m. for Belvedere, a summit recommended for boys of ten and twelve. This was the seventeenth time we were going to vanquish it. For there was no doubt in our minds as to the final victory. My brother and I made a good team, a solid roped party. We weren't afraid of the Lac Blanc, nor of the névé jutting out above it, nor of the final climb even though there was a danger of a fifty and then a one hundred and fifty foot fall. However, there was the departure at night. This was certainly the most difficult aspect of the adventure. Sixteen times already we had set out at three o'clock. My brother never understood the necessity of such an early departure since we usually returned when Chamonix's summer visitors were eating breakfast. Alpinists always set out at night. It certainly was not up to us, at our tender age, to change the rules. Then too, why did he have sigh about the weight of our knapsacks? One can't go off without taking into account the possibility of a storm, the condition of the ice or rock which can sometimes be catastrophic for want of a small object like an ice-axe, a warm cap, or a climbing iron. It's true we didn't have real climbing-irons and our substitutes for them were clumsy and heavy; it's true that our knapsacks were rather enormous, but prudence is the serious Alpinist's first commandment. My brother was a bit young to understand such things! Alpinists very obviously don't have the opportunity for a breakfast of hot chocolate or creamy coffee with bread and butter. I tried to make my brother understand this as we ate some canned sardines in olive oil before leaving home. Outside it was pitch dark and, admittedly, rather awesome. We spoke in low voices instinctively and soon fell silent. It was the same every time. Through the pines we could see thousands of stars glittering; the Milky Way, the Big Dipper, stars whose names were unknown to us. I could distinguish the outlines of mountains in regions of the sky which were starless. The silence, especially, was oppressive. Our feet would slip on stones in the path; we could hear each other breathing. There were strange rustling noises and the distant rumbling of the Arve River. I was struck, as always, by the perfume of pine resin and mountain flowers; it was as if the flowers breathed more freely at night, as if a secret complicity had sprung up between them and the phantasms we had become. During those night outings, in which my mind was gradually invaded by nature's enormous presence, I always had the impression of being the dream the plants were having—a great flower which moved, a small, ambulant pine tree—of being also a huge beast for the little ones which fled at my approach or stood rooted to the spot, petrified by fear as my gigantic foot squashed thousands of lives. I was nature crushing nature. And I strove to make my steps no less heavy for fear of setting off a universal cataclysm by transgressing immemorial laws. My foot had to fall as it would and nothing could sway its murderous course except perhaps a stone which could make me stumble, probably placed there to protect a privileged kingdom. Sometimes it was a big rock which I blundered into with a surprised grunt, or a pine tree, or animals bigger than I which stopped me brutally in my tracks. I would swear, but so quietly that my brother could scarcely hear me, intent as he was, like me, on disturbing nothing in the implacable order and silence which is the law of the mountain at night, the first rule which must be followed blindly.

Above the timber line, day was breaking while we followed the regular course of a stream whose murmur guided our steps. Then, as through a suddenly opened curtain, we escaped from the night's spell and assumed our individuality; we chose our path in a nature which was now merely a setting, until another night, another communion.
Can I say that I liked the mountain in those moments of trance? Does one love one's reflection in a mirror? I was the mountain, I was a part of it and all of it, that which crushes and is crushed, breaking down the already open doors of night.

Even today that question has no meaning. I like the mountain because it smells of resin. As one's mouth waters on hearing certain appetizing words, so my nostrils are filled with the perfume of resin on hearing the word "mountain," the true, perceptible, substantial odor, like the good pine tree that I have remained.

★

DURING THE YEARS preceding our successive, always successful attacks on Belvedere, we spent our vacation in a small village of the Bossons in that same Chamonix valley. Surrounded by meadows, by woods which concealed the sharp peaks, the countryside was pleasant enough and our vacations would have passed calmly had we not been extremely conscious of the close proximity of a natural, astounding phenomenon, of a gigantic monster slumbering behind a curtain of trees just a few minutes walk from our house: a glacier. A glacier, a colossal which mass sprawled right up to the gates of the village. A real glacier with green and blue crevasses, a clean, white, smooth glacier sending sparkling lights into the sky. Ice in mid-summer, as slippery as the frozen ponds in winter, just as amusing but much more exciting since the game consisted precisely in avoiding glissades present at every step. From the most rudimentary way of placing one foot before the other, to the defiance hurled at the slope by attacking it in the regions least promising of success, there are degrees of temptation to be explored one by one with the paradoxical spirit of a curio collector. After discovering this prodigious glacier, I was to make it the center of my childhood vacations for two or three years, every single day during the three month summer vacation, whatever the weather, with an obstinacy which still amazes me today. I have always been convinced that by staring for whole days at a simple cork one could finally, if one didn't slip into acute melancholia first, discover all the secrets of the universe. I can't estimate to within a hundred how many times I took that narrow path through an alder woods which led me in twenty minutes to the edge of the mastodon. Three hundred, four hundred times... always eager, my heart pounding, I would approach that colossal lollipop offered by the mountain. I would begin by gravely considering that strange substance which the mountain had dumped from on high and the thoughts which that overwhelming bulk inspired in me were nothing short of morose. By its proportions, the world I beheld replaced my condition of a human being struggling in a material world of infinite destructive possibilities, with conditions which were its own: an extraordinary vulnerability. Nothing can prevent water from freezing when it is meant to freeze, nothing could have prevented the entire planet and all that lives on it from becoming petrified for ever and ever if the moment had come. As proof of that fabulous, horrible truth I had before my eyes those billions of frozen tons under a summer sun, substance convulsed by a long agony, offered for my contemplation as a precedent, an example, as a menace.

Reckoning with earthy optimism that this menace would not be put into execution that very day, I would determinedly put my foot down on it without the least reaction on the monster's part. It did not budge. The moment obviously had not yet arrived.

Then, considering the composition of ice, inert ice, I would smile on thinking of the notions that unenlightened boys my age had about ice. Verily, ice is not ice. There is ice and ice just as there are sheep and sheep, men and men. It is smooth or granular, it is crumbly or compact, opaque or transparent, white or gray or black, green, blue, moiré, flat or wavy like the desert sands; it can have rounded, feminine forms or be sharp and pointed, it conceals in its entrails its own precipices, dizzy crevasses, green, then blue, then black, unpleasant to see, its peaks, its towers with scintillating, vertical sides, its plains with their calm contrasts and its seas of high waves, its superficial torrents twisting in arabesques, its pools of a thousand shades of pearly jade, rose and sapphire, its underground rivers whose low rumbling does not disturb the crystalline murmur of the surface waters which moan feebly as they solidify or bubble forth with sharp little cries when they are freed and recover their fluidity over which they seem so uncertain that they run off awkwardly, helter-skelter, as if panic-stricken.

It is a complete, self-sufficient universe which, in spite of its gigantism, made me wonder why it had stopped there, why it hadn't overflowed its banks, sending its tentacles over valleys and plains, rivers and seas, to cover the whole globe, to annex the universe, along with me, including me, a me petrified in the form of a statue which I sometimes caught myself recognizing in a particularly noble-looking ice pinnacle.

Of course I had not lost interest in the problems of moving about on such diversified matter; I learned to know its mechanical reactions, it became familiar to me; but I sought above all else, and with all my energy, to understand it, to go to the very heart of its suffering. It was certainly for me a moaning thing, crushed, compressed, hammered, terrorized by an ineffable monster, but still living and awaiting a prince-liberator who would break the spell with his sincere love. I would have liked to have been that prince and I was stung by a sort of guilt on feeling myself so obviously inadequate. I wanted to attenuate that guilty conscience by doing everything in my power, my ridiculous little power, by offering my presence. I wanted, in all events, to be faithful. And I truly was. Every day I was there and though I may have done acrobatics while climbing hundreds of yards up the glacier, it was to observe the transformations in a crevasse whose walls were especially compact, black, as if dying, with lips each day more pinched or, to the contrary, more relaxed, a fearsome wound which I examined in silence since I was unable to bandage it. On the way I noted the collapse of an ice pinnacle, the caprices of a small gully which each day lengthened its course by a crevasse, stooping over a spiral pot-hole, no longer in use, but still dizzily intoxicating. It was my world. It was, in any case, my summer vacation, every day of my vacation, a life within a life.

★

THE YEARS passed and after having flirted with the Bossons glacier, taken myself for a pine tree and conquered the Belvedere seventeen to nothing, my steps chanced to lead me to the foot of granite rocks. I had grown up too much to identify myself with the first pinnacle along the way but I was just as intimately related to the rock. The word "rock" calls to mind, I believe, an idea of effort, of danger. It was for me essentially a contact, a form which fits the palm of the hand. Whether smooth skin or rough skin, sharp ridge, trenchant blades or rounded branch, delicate, pudgy or humped reliefs, I experienced a disconcerting pleasure in touching, grasping, slipping along, clasping with my hands, fingers, whole body. Warm, colorful substance so rarely treacherous, always willing and ready for pleasure. Of course climbing seems to be an effort but that orgy of muscular explosions is above all a practically boundless intoxication, a universe of tactile sensations in which the mind loses its empire. Later when I became a real Alpinist with real cords, real climbing-irons, modern equipment in ultra-light knapsacks, the voluptuousness of the contact with granite was never supplanted by the satisfaction of banally reaching an artificially fixed goal.

★

LIKE ALL my Alpinist friends, I have traveled through the Alps, its prolongations or its fabulous expansions; the Himalayas I have often walked in the night; I have gone up glaciers, climbed cliffs, but nothing essentially new came to modify what was given to me in the beginning. The roots which bind me to every form of mountain are too deep for me to find their exact source. I cannot stand to one side and watch myself go by and, even if I could, I would only perceive, mixed together in a singular vision, the pine trees of the Alps, granite lace, towers of blue ice, a world of lofty clouds.

MAURICE HERZOG

IN THE DAYS when propeller planes still served Polynesia they disembarked their passengers from Paris on the coral of Bora Bora.

There the poor souls, dazed by a journey of three days and as many nights, bewildered by the changing time-zones, dazzled by the tropical sun, blinded by the scintillating lagoon, were led to a shed on the edge of the landing strip. And what met their eyes in the shelter's semidarkness, in the midst of a mob of half-naked girls and flower-wreathed boys, in the racket of Hawaiian guitars and Maori chants? A very classic French Railway poster of Mont Blanc.

With one of the most beautiful landscapes of the Leeward Islands' archipelago before their eyes, the people of Oceania found no more fitting tribute to the Old World than that picture of the Alps.

★

A HAPPY CHOICE, we thought two months later on seeing Mont Blanc looming up out of a gorge, the Servoz Gorge.

Mont Blanc, divested of its habitual vapors, its youth restored by the Bora Bora poster, a heap of forests, meadows, rocks, ice, snow and sky, both dumbfounding and harmonious, was truly one of the wonders of this world.

Victor Hugo didn't share our enthusiasm and his treatment of the Servoz valley was very offhand. He wrote, "The Sallanches valley is a theater." He later wrote, "The Chamonix valley is a temple." It is true that the law of contrasts, so dear to the Romantics, forced him to make this gloomy comparison: "The Servoz valley is a tomb."

May Servoz forgive him. Poetry is an exacting mistress.

It was Charles Nodier who, in 1825, led Hugo to the foot of Mont Blanc. He had looked

Antiquity lodged the gods on the mountain tops. The Middle Ages raised them to the sky and installed the demons on the peaks. Finally, better exorcist than the monks, modern man, obstinate and restless, chased the Olympians and devils from the sparkling ridges and gloomy crevasses.
And yet someone still remained.
The White Lady of the Glaciers? The Mother Goddess of Snow?
She reigns, statue of stone, colossus dressed in storm clouds, airy silhouette, fragile design in ice. Between Romansh and Veneon, it is the most beautiful mountain in France, the Alpinists' sacred peak, the unique Meije. From the Our Lady of the Snow chapel one can see on the crest of the Grand Pic, the Finger of God watching over the Mouth of Man.
Spring and Autumn make her more beautiful still, looming up in the azure blue, always sparkling clean as if after a storm. She fascinates the astonished traveler. Some have died for her, a fulgurating death in space, or slowly in frozen agony. He who contemplates her at night, hardy, shivering man camping out, or tourist behind a window of the Hotel du Chazelet, if he sees her haloed between two streaks of clouds, clearly senses that she is not merely a mountain but the symbol of beauty all too rare.

forward to seeing his friend's amazement but he narrowly missed being disappointed, for the giant of the Alps did not deign to bare its head before the giant of the poets.

Nevertheless, Hugo gave it the "full organ" treatment. He spoke of cathedrals, obelisks, alabaster frontons, pearly pilasters, of icy tiaras and mantles of snow.

Hugo, the iconoclast, the enemy of prejudices, owed it to himself to rehabilitate such a disreputable, disparaged mountain.

Indeed, for ages the Alps had been thought of as a mound of stones flung into the middle of Europe for the sole purpose of hindering the advance of armies.

The traveler who ventured into the region saw only terrifying chasms and steep slopes which defied good taste as well as good sense.

Occasionally the complaints made against it were more original. In 1699, a visitor reproached it for not being conducive to hiking. Six years later a learned professor attacked the air breathed in Switzerland and Tyrol. It appeared that its vivacity could make one idiotic.

In 1726 an authentic scientist wrote a description, complete with illustrations, of the different species of dragons to be encountered in Alpine valleys.

The eighteenth century, however, gave these "crude" mountains dignity. After being an object of terror, the Alps became a subject for study. Theories were put forth. Sometimes very strange ones. There was thought to be, confined in the bottom of a crypt, an immense ocean of ice which fed through seracs and crevasses all the glaciers of Switzerland and Savoy.

Then the poets joined in and those singers of Nature, carried away by their own flights of fancy, went so far as to compare the granite needles and cascades of snow to cardboard stage scenery.

★

Distant places are seen nearer through a telescope of leaves. A sight is needed to aim at the exact spot where the snow and sky shimmer with heat and melt in the southern sun.
Whether a springtime or an autumn tree, it looks the same outlined against the Himalayas at Darjeeling, against Mont Blanc seen from Sallanches, and in this case against the Belledonne in Dauphiné.

The troubadour, Albertet de Sisteron, would still recognize his hometown in spite of the bridge whose modern arch straddles the Durance River. As in the Middle Ages, the houses are squeezed between the cliff and the river and the gardens are still hanging on skimpy plots of earth imposed on the mountain by low walls.

What kind of headdresses of stone and water are these young ladies wearing? From what sky comes that millinery rain which never falls and yet torments and shifts the sand and polishes the rock? From what planet do these monsters come or from what era are these mummies?
It is not wise to spend the night in this region where worlds come together or a door opens, perhaps, on some terrifying secret recess in the Universe.
The high altitudes, like the heaths, have their Red Inns, their Salems, and their petrified wives of Lot.

This country has a legendary name: Guillaume Peyrouse and Clemence d'Ambel. A love story: but administrative love. Chapelle-en-Valgaudemar is the hamlet where, in the joint townhall, are kept the records and plan of the Siamese-twin parishes of Guillaume Peyrouse and Clemence d'Ambel.

The lower valley where a torrent of pebbles flows resembles the mountain ridges from which the glaciers, worn out by the sun, gradually melt away.

In this end-of-the-world scenery, it is pleasant to imagine a Guillaume Peyrouse, a poor shepherd, lifting his eyes to a nearby yet inaccessible Clemence.

THE IDEA of Alpine picturesqueness has entered into our thinking.

In appearance, at least, for in actual fact, the mountain has not yet won the affection of the masses.

With the sea there is no hesitation. But those peaks, only yesterday considered frightful, do not enjoy the same privilege.

No one in a social gathering would take it into his head to declare that the view of the ocean overpowered him. But if you exclaim, "The Chamonix valley oppresses me," or "The sight of the Matterhorn makes me feel depressed," your reputation won't suffer.

What is the reason for this hostility? A mountain does not lend itself to sunbathing.

It can't be loved passively, in a wallowing way. It can be cherished from an invalid's chaise longue but that kind of love demands still more effort, if only an effort of the imagination.

The passion which the Alps inspire is always based on a curiosity of the mind, on a desire to go see what it's like on top or beyond that ridge.

Why was Mont Blanc the first tall peak in the Alps to be conquered? Because it was the highest? No. If it had been hidden in the heart of a lonely mountain range no one in the eighteenth century would have thought of climbing it. But its peak was visible from Geneva and a young man from that city, Horace-Bénédict de Saussure, was tempted.

One day in 1760, he set out for those glaciers which had so fascinated him. He was only twenty but he would need all the enthusiasm of his youth to undertake a voyage which was still an expedition.

At Sallanches the carriage-road ended and a cart-road in very bad condition began.

On reaching the hamlet of "Chamouni" the young man discovered that his troubles were not over. The beds there were as hard as the roadside and he was obliged to borrow the priest's bed.

A shepherd and his dog take a moment's rest while keeping an alert eye on the flock.
A delivery boy sets out with the groceries for a refuge.
A roped party following its guide, its Premier, trudges slowly away, dragging its multiple shadow over the burning glacier.
All these men — whether the man of the Alps, of the first moraine, or those of the geological highroad — are well acquainted with the weight of the sky, the miserliness of the earth, the cost of each step.
On the balcony, prisoners behind a barrier, the non-participants of the Aiguille du Midi and its step-saving funicular, now seated at the banquet table of the Alps, look uncomprehendingly at this universe which they have not earned.

These inconveniences didn't in the least discourage Horace-Bénédict. He promised a "rather large" reward to anyone finding a way of reaching the top of Mont Blanc.

Rock-crystal and chamois hunters began to explore the mountain.

The task was not easy, alas. Monsieur de Saussure returned to Geneva, was named Professor of Philosophy, got married, visited Paris, Holland, England, and Italy, climbed Mount Etna, had three children, and Mont Blanc was still unvanquished.

An incident was to bring about victory.

On June 8, 1786, the guide Jacques Balmat from Pèlerins, a village near Chamonix, returning home after an unsuccessful attempt to reach the top, was forced to spend the night outside on a glacier. In the morning he was shivering but, to his great astonishment, still alive. The evil spirits of the mountain had not taken advantage of the darkness to make off with him.

That was the end of a stubborn superstition. Thereafter, the conquest was imminent, for the assault on the highest peak in the Alps could be undertaken in stages while camping out.

Indeed, on August 8, 1786, at 6:23 p.m., Balmat and a doctor from the valley, Michel Gabriel Paccard, set foot on the snowy summit.

Now it was up to Monsieur de Saussure to crown his work by climbing Mont Blanc himself. This he did on August 3, 1787. But the battle had been too long and tedious and on reaching the top the gentleman from Geneva trampled the snow in a fit of rage in front of Balmat and the seventeen other guides and the servant who had accompanied him.

Jacques Balmat reaped many benefits from his exploit. M. de Saussure handed over the promised reward. The king of Sardinia allowed him to call himself Balmat alias Mont Blanc. The emperor Napoleon made him a tax collector. As for Alexandre Dumas, he conferred on him the

The lake is an impressionist painter. The mountain trembles occasionally, like this reflection, in the paintings by Gustave Doré, Linck, or Calame. From the background of the Mona Lisa *to the* Mont Blanc Seen From the Faucille *by Rousseau, the strokes are timid as if the model were dissolving in the artist's paints. There is a curse on the relationship between art and the architecture of the peaks. The same ostracism excludes the altitude from poetry. Yet Dante warned us that "del mondo consacro Jeova le cime." Could Divine Harmony be more elusive than the divine? It's true that it is not created in our image. Unless, as André Gide suggested, the mountain is a product of protestantism. An unthinking iconoclasm would then leave to nature alone the task of shaping the face of the planet.*

But taboos are unknown to the camera. Finding a reflective lake, where the depths of the summits find rest, it recaptures the sources of inspiration.

whimsical title of "The Christopher Columbus of the Alps".

The valley has changed a lot since those distant times and, yet, one still comes across old guides at Chamonix who could have been the brothers of that Balmat-Mont-Blanc.

Their step is sure and their words rare. If the client following them asks what the weather will be like, they reply, "Keep going." Exhausted, the client cries for mercy and the guides don't even turn around to utter their "Keep going." The client is offended by this rough encouragement in the form of an order and rails against the rude bunch of people in Chamonix.

"Keep going," is the only explanation he'll receive.

And then, at the end of the journey, the client realizes that their "Keep going," is not an order but a pat expression used in Savoy, a laconic country, when there is nothing else to say.

Hardworking and close with their money, the old inhabitants of Chamonix have all the virtues of those who till the soil with an extra ingredient, whimsy, which leads sensible men into the wildest adventures.

Balmat-Mont-Blanc could have basked in his fame and the fortune that his fame brought. Not at all! At seventy-two he was still roaming the mountainside. It was no longer in search of a route through a maze of crevasses. Another passion had taken hold of him: gold, a very hypothetical gold which, according to legend, was thought to be mixed in with the rock-crystal and quartz of a few high valleys.

The "Fer à Cheval" (Horseshoe) is a calciferous circus rising out of the vale of Sixtus. It is a solitary spot although always inhabited by the roar of cascades—in summer there are more than thirty of them—falling down over the cliffs.

In this austere setting one day in September 1834, Jacques Balmat obstinately followed a narrow cornice leading into the mountainside.

Like the world, the Dauphiné region has its Seven Wonders: the Fontaine Ardente (Burning Fountain), the Tour-sans-Venin (Venomless Tower), the Montagne Inaccessible (the Inaccessible Mountain), the Cuves de Sassenage (Vats of Sassenage), the Manne de Briançon (Briançon Breadbasket), the Pré qui Tremble (Trembling Meadow), Grotte de Notre-Dame de la Balme. Whoever drew up the list forgot one: the Ecrins (Jewel Boxes).

Hidden away in the central mountain mass of Upper Dauphiné the Ecrins, Tête Noire and Tête Blanche thrust themselves 14,000 *feet in the air: they are the lords of Romansh, Veneon and Briançon.*

Their sky is the sky of Greece or of Sicily. There, perhaps, even now exists an Olympia.

But whether gods of black stone or gods of ice, in winter as in summer, we prefer them rooted to the spot, frozen stiff, statues in an arena awaiting the gladiators of High Altitude.

June 27, 1492

Pointing to the West, Columbus' caravels will leave Palos soon to land on the shores of an unknown continent.
The French army crosses Dauphiné on the order of Charles VIII whose royal will makes even nature bow down. Antoine de Ville, lord of Domjulien and Beaupré, captain of Montélimar, chamberlain, after a two-day battle against space and fear, reaches the top of Mons Inencensibilis.
Like Columbus and America, he unwittingly invented Alpinism and offered men an unexpected continent: high altitude.
And Rabelais marveled that under such conditions one could climb up such a "pumpkin."
Mont Aiguille is no longer inaccessible but it still puts up a very good fight.
Today not one virgin peak remains in the Alps. Five centuries were sufficient to write this history, unlike History, which is the Alpine Epic.
Even around the crumbling Aiguille Noire, not even the tiniest peak or rock pinnacle remains to be conquered.

His companion saw him disappear behind a rock. He waited for him in vain. The old guide never returned. In spite of search parties his body was never recovered.

His friends and family had one consolation at least: Balmat-Mont-Blanc had found a death worthy of him.

During this time Mont Blanc had come into fashion. It was even on the brink of taking a fiancée of very good family. On September 3, 1838, Mademoiselle Henriette d'Angeville undertook its ascension. She wanted to be the second woman to attain that illustrious summit, the first being Marie Paradis, an inn servant whom the guides had dragged more than led to the top in 1808.

Mlle d'Angeville had fallen in love with Mont Blanc while gazing at it from her castle window in the Bugey valley. But that romantic lady was also methodical. She had foreseen everything including the worst, for she drew up her will. And dressed in a pair of wide homespun pants "with a bib above and gaiters below fitting into her shoes," she entrusted her porters with a fan, a brush, a coffeepot, a pillow, a shoehorn, a small mirror "to set her bonnet straight" and a homing pigeon to announce victory.

All this care almost proved useless. Having reached a place called the "Grand Plateau," Henriette swooned. Would it be necessary to hoist her to the top? No. Mlle d'Angeville was not another Marie Paradis. She stood up, exclaiming with the eloquence of her day, "If I die before reaching the top, drag my body up there and leave it."

She did not die and reached the summit. But once there what did she discover? Despite a few stone-falls, the peak of Mont Blanc has not changed much since Mlle d'Angeville's ascension. In good weather it is disappointing. What? That steep peak is only this? A snowy plateau devoid of beauty. A waste land, we almost

Pelvoux and Ailefroide are lying in ambush in the clouds, the White Glacier creeps along, an icy moat defending crenelated walls.
This mountain mass is a nook in the Alps. Far from everything, away from the beaten track, between Champsaur and Vallouise, it leans against Savoy, protecting it from the raging storms which descend from Mont Blanc, shrugging them off in order to keep the sky blue over the southern Alps.

The black sky of the heights looks down on the earth's cathedrals: Mont Blanc and its satellites. Lower still are islands. Islands of water surrounded by an ocean of rock.

wrote. It doesn't even make one dizzy. It is too vast.

As for the view from it, it is only a panorama such as is seen from a plane, nothing more. Mont Blanc is a victim of its isolation and altitude. It is too dominating.

However, don't rely too much on its good-natured appearance. It takes very little for it to assume a tragic beauty. A threat is enough: a cloud rising, fog creeping in, a sky clouding over and, suddenly, this debonair slope becomes the most alarming ridge imaginable.

An end of the world on high.

Tragedies up there are countless, it is true. On that inviting snow, men have died of the cold and others of burns from lightning bolts.

But Mont Blanc's duality as both Sunday hiking grounds and a death peak makes up its charm, a charm that bewitches even the cautious.

★

THE TUNNEL diggers, the builders of overhead tramways, have given the Chamonix valley a different appearance but there is a high spot in the valley which has not changed since the time of the good Monsieur Perrichon.

At Montenvert, in the shadow of the famous needles, the same dumbfounded crowds gather on summer days. They continue to show off their brand new climbing outfits before the scornful Dru peak, venturing forth cautiously onto the Sea of Ice, thinking to tread on one of the marvels of the mountain.

It is a gully-hole really, for although glaciers are pure and beautiful at their source, they become flat, gray and dirty at the outfall. The stones spewed out by the crevasses make them veritable dumps.

Let's be fair—one has only to lift his eyes to find the sublime, an architecture of needles, peaks,

Where there's a Will
... there's a Way.

ridges, suspended ice-pinnacles which no human imagination could have conceived.

The Montenvert has received illustrious visitors in every era. Paul Payot, the historian of Mont-Blanc, tells us that the Empress Josephine went there in 1819, incognito, recently divorced, but rather conspicuous nonetheless since sixty-eight guides watched over her.

In the refuge's album, pompously named "The Temple of Nature", she wrote these lines:

"*Ah! I sense that, in the midst of these great wonders,*
These touching scenes, this awesome sight,
Our spirit is possessed, our eyes called heavenward.
The heart, alone for a moment, finds rest in this place."

It was a plagiarism. The imperial visitor had simply imitated a poem by Delille, who had visited the spot a few years earlier.

The Montenvert was to offer Josephine another joy. This ardent botanist discovered between two pebbles a tuft of *Linnaea Borealis*, an extremely rare plant.

Unfortunately, the next day an awkward peasant revealed to her that it was he, on the orders of a fawning chemist, who had placed the precious plant on her path. Josephine had the good sense to laugh at this piece of trickery. She even gave the peasant some money to reward him for his frankness and for his morning's walk.

Until 1908, the most common means of transportation to Montenvert was the mule. And an officially approved mule, at that! Every fifteenth of May all mule candidates were gathered at Chamonix in the church square and submitted to an examination by a committee presided over by the justice of peace of Saint-Gervais. Any animal showing a tendency to be short-winded, disobedient, skittish, myopic, subject to dizziness or mountain sickness, in brief, who was not sure-footed and clear-sighted, was sent back to his stable.

Approved mules were an appreciable source of revenue since they received six francs for each

In hidden nooks there are laboratories and dispensaries where the sky and the weather carry out black magic. The mountain is gnawed to the bone. Its skeleton is bare. Unless it is viscera instead.
The clouds, born of the glacier which is suspended from the Aiguille du Tacul and the Col des Hirondelles, cluster together to conceal this nightmare. The ice is gray! It has been soiled by all the residue of rocks, meteors or dust falling for thousands and thousands of years from the flanks of the mountains and which the glacier slowly digests, pushing the blocks millimeter by millimeter towards the distant frontal moraine.
It's an experience to sit on the peaceful terrace of the Montenvers station and see the ice torrent which the Romantics called the Sea. It must be seen when the air is full of ozone, when the storm clouds gather, moving up the side of the Drus peaks and attacking the three thousand feet of ice on the Grandes Jorasses. Then, even if one knows, as any good geologist would, that these frozen waves are the product of the glacier's flow and friction on the broken layers of its bed, one can't help thinking that the storm is the true woodcutter who strikes, chops and saws.

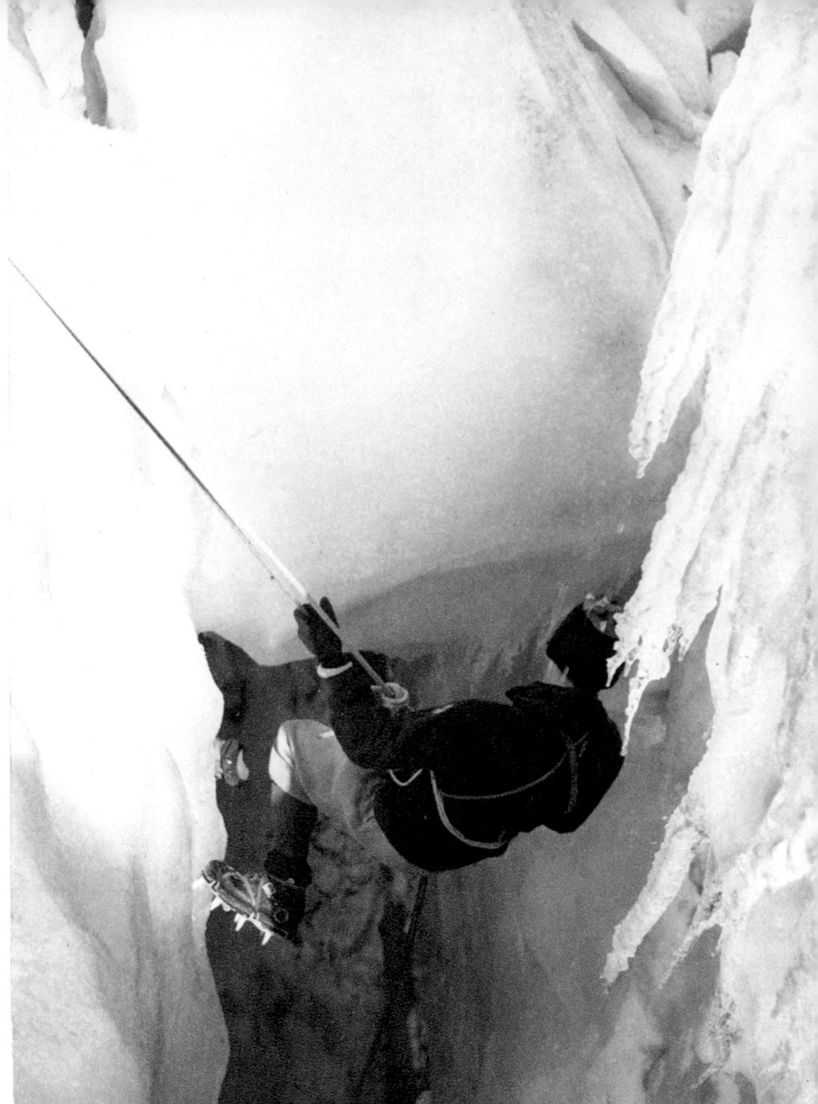

The cosmonaut of the vertical and the altitude — of the attitude, a joker would say — in that state of imponderability more psychological than sporting, is a funambulist who is judged by the initiated according to the rites of the piton and the stirrups, the ballet of the doubled rope, the games of the glacier's labyrinth, the yoga of ascensional creeping. Ardent admirers of cliff scaling, they encourage the empty-handed pygmies who dare to brave the giants.

trip. Consequently, a misogynous municipality forbade renting them "to the weaker sex or to children under fifteen years of age."

In 1908, the little rack railway was inaugurated. Its locomotives were equipped with all the latest inventions. Just think: a brake automatically stopped the machine when it exceeded six miles an hour.

The track is still the same today. To go up to Montenvert it still passes through, on its three-mile journey, a spiral tunnel called the "Grépon Tunnel" and over a few viaducts. But electricity has replaced steam.

The cars of this miniature train are one of the rare places where the climber may come in contact with the hiker, one saddled with equipment, the other scantily clad, one in a warm jacket, the other in shorts, one setting out on an expedition, the other just out for a little stroll.

Such confrontations bring out the peculiarities and absurdities of each.

In the presence of a tourist, an Alpinist, even if he has only just left his desk in Paris, won't say, "It will be sunny tomorrow," but "Tomorrow will be a dilly." He won't exclaim, "I hung onto a rock," but "I seized a hold." Is a certain passage easy? The scornful, categorical reply, "It's for the cows," or in other words, a cowpath.

The tourist, on the other hand, asks one ridiculous question after another.

In one of those cars during a momentary *entente cordiale* we heard a lady ask as she pointed to the Dru:

"Hasn't anyone ever climbed that mountain over there?"

"Yes, it's been climbed."

Stupefied, she added, "Oh, really? Is there a path?"

A path! If the poor woman could have seen the overhanging chimneys, the inch-wide crevasses, the vertical slabs of rock, the blades as smooth as glass by which Mummery and his

A chat on the Nantillons Pass at 10,000 and some feet.
In the black and white world, the guide — Gaston Rebuffat — and client consult each other.
It is not a question of itinerary but of philosophy. What is clear: is it the black or the white?
There is no answer to this when morning breaks and the sun skims over the crevasses' unfathomable depths... Unless it is evening instead...
The mountain, which makes us dizzy, has dizzy spells itself and, like shadow and light, confuses night with day.

Xor incostrati muta eius custos carzeris dicta zor nominat oratione
martiris incliti sabastiani ad loglam redit

Raw stone has its own handwriting which, alongside the granite carved by the wind and the centuries, is inscribed on blocks polished by hands and hours.
It can burst into warm colors in the sun of the Assy plateau ; it can be faintly phosphorescent like the old Saint Anthony of Bessans, sheltered by the overhanging tiles.
It is a prayer book on stone parchments recounting human suffering in the midst of the Alps' heaving landscapes. Doesn't the Saint Sebastian of Lanslevillard, painted for the spiritual edification of the faithful, evoke the martyrdom of the world above him, of that geological soul which is also menaced by a thousand arrows from the creative infinite ?
All high places have their limits, a frontier which can be crossed only at the risk of getting lost. The cross is planted there like a signal, like the prayer of a Nevache peasant. It is made of wood, facing the rocks, just as it was designed during Saint Louis' reign. Beyond the naive symbols of the Passion, a world exists which is no longer on a human scale but on God's.

followers passed and still pass, she would have been struck speechless.

A.F. Mummery, who was in the second half of the nineteenth century the first "acrobatic Alpinist"—to use his own term—was a thin Englishman wearing a pince-nez and a drooping mustache on his hatchet face.

You are already imagining an apprehensive civil servant, but you're mistaken. Never have the Alps known a more furious climber. He once wrote, "Even if there were nothing to see, I'd keep on climbing."

He is considered the father of modern Alpinism. In his private life this innovator was less ahead of his time. The intrepid pioneer was also timid and bound by all the prejudices of his day.

One day he paid a visit to his favorite guide, Burgener, but the latter could not receive him. He was in bed. No, he wasn't sick, but his pants were torn. During a climb he had ripped them and had been obliged to send them to the tailor even though he didn't have a second pair.

One would think that Mummery would have entered the bedroom of the guide with whom he had shared so many hopes and fears, so many troubles and labors. No, his dignity would not allow him to do so. He sent another guide to talk to Burgener.

Let's forget these little failings. For an Alpinist, Mummery is and will always remain the vanquisher of the Grépon. What is the Grépon anyway? An ice-covered giant? We'll see by it's altitude that there are many higher. Mont Blanc towers 15,781 feet above sea level, the Matterhorn 14,780 feet, the Aiguille Verte 13,520 feet, and the Grépon 11,424 feet. There is no snow on top and luckily so for its narrow platform cannot hold more than eight men.

Why, then, did the Grépon, mere needle of Chamonix, have such a reputation? Because, since Balmat, times had changed. It had become less a question of a height to be conquered than

From his hut on stilts, built on what was later to be called the "Annecy Cove," a prehistoric creature looked fearfully into the distance at the earth and the tangled clouds which formed a magic sky. Two-legged animals with agile hands had set up an advance station there from which the look-outs could spy on the top ranking entities of lightning and thunder. Since those unremembered days nothing has changed in the landscape. The houses, like the city, are lacustrine, with a wooden pier to protect the boats. The lake is still the last station, the halt before the solemn entrance into the high, wreathed valleys.

a difficulty to be overcome. Now, Grépon, a rock icicle all of a piece presents terrible difficulties on its flanks.

Would you like proof? Mummery reached the top of the Grépon on August 5, 1881. He left his ice-axe there, promising a 1,000 franc reward to anyone who could bring it back to him. It was only after four years that an officer of the Alpine Ski Troops, Henri Dunod, succeeded in recovering the stake.

Dunod's guide expected to receive the promised 1,000 francs but Mummery refused, saying, "The offer was good only for a season."

Was Mummery something short of a gentleman? In any case, his death wipes out the memory of his pettiness. He perished, carried off by an avalanche in the Himalayas at the foot of Nanga Parbat, and the mountain, as in the case of Jacques Balmat, refused to give up his body.

Today the Grépon has become a "ladies' mountain," an exercise for beginning climbers. In good weather people line up to climb the trail opened up by Mummery.

On these abrupt cliffs, in addition to the sheer joy of climbing, is another pleasure, that of finding all the passages to which the struggles of Mummery and his guides gave names.

There are no anonymous walls here. One "chimney sweeps" the *Mummery*, crosses the *Trou du Canon* (Cannon's Mouth), crawls along the *Rateau de Chèvre* (Goat's Rake), descends the *Grand Gendarme* (Big Policeman), edges along the *Vire aux Bicyclettes* (Bicycle Track), and finally reaches the top by the *Fissure terminale en Z* (Z-shaped Terminal Fissure).

Only one mountain bears on its ridges and walls names as mysteriously poetic, the Meije in Oisans, which a twenty-year-old French boy, Boileau de Castelnau, destined for an early death, was to climb on August 16, 1877.

In a dreary student's room, staring blankly at

The Green Needle and the Nameless.
The Dense Ones.
The ecclesiastical ridge with its Cardinal, its Nun and its Monk.
The Little and Great Jorasses separated by Swallows' Pass.
Rochefort Ridge overlooking the Tacul Needle, the Angle and the Sea of Ice.
Such are the names of these mountains, of these marvels which these two tourists, impatient to ski, choose to ignore, turning their backs on them, passengers of Flégère's aerial egg.

*All sailors are not old salt.
nor all mountaineers professional climbers. The thre
great seas of the Wester
Alps — Annecy, Le Bourget
Lake Geneva — all hav
their Rivieras. The sun shine
there, all the warmer fo
being reflected on the snow
peaks. The thawed snow lie
quietly, warm to naked bodies
Spring water is wholesom
even if Verlaine never taste
it, preferring — during a
extraordinary cure at Ai
— a "sourish" wine whic
went down more easily.*

a Greek or Latin dictionary, how many uncounted boys have dreamed of the *Glacier Carré* (Square Glacier), of the *Pas de Chat* (Cat's Step), of the *Fauteuil* (Armchair), of the *Cheval Rouge* (Red Horse), of the *Dos de l'Ane* (Donkey's Back), of the *Petit Doigt* and *Grand Doigt* (Little Finger and Big Finger), of the *Z*, of the *Couloir du Crapaud* (Toad's Passage). How many vocations have sprung from such dreams?

On the other side of the wall, his parents were reassured. The boy was working. And even if he did let his mind wander a little it wasn't serious.

The poor people didn't realize that a passion had caught hold of their son, a passion which might lead him up the beaten track to mountain peaks, but a passion which could also lead him to wild adventure, for mountain climbing has become a Game of Death.

Some people, however, are perplexed by youths who risk their lives for nothing.

Mummery replied in advance in the name of such youths. Mummery, who wanted to forbid the mountain to scientists and poets and to reserve it exclusively for sportsmen, wrote, "Great ascensions sometimes require sacrifice but the true man of the mountain does not renounce his passion even if he knows he is the chosen victim."

One day in the month of August, 1932, two "true men of the mountain" were climbing the Couloir Couturier on the north side of the Aiguille Verte, a veritable icy toboggan slide, a mile of perpendicular rock ending in the crevasses of the Argentières glacier.

Greloz and Valluet had almost reached the top of this chute when a small avalanche knocked them from the steps they had chopped out of the ice to climb. Then came the terrifying, dizzy fall such as a man of the city could never imagine: falling down the height of three Eiffel Towers, crashing against outcropping rocks along the way.

This cartoon showing the same person outlined on the peak, in the gap, or hanging in mid-air, illustrates the industriousness of an ant. The dizzy sugar-loaf is only the Aiguillete d'Argentière, the kindergarten of mountain climbing.
However, behind it lurks another world: Mont Blanc and its needles where climbing is no longer child's play.

5

Skiing is a military sport. It imposes the discipline of the classroom and marching. Going up, families are packed by the square inch into the funicular ; on the downward journey, stakes, crowds and crevasses mark out the trails it is advisable to follow.

In the sunny winter blast, wind-burned faces grow brown in the heat and cold. The secret of the snow's success is this transmutation from frost into fire.

Skiing is the sport which makes man feel the freest.

Even in championships, the skier speeding between the gates and toward the flags, traces his trail, designs the slalom which, like his handwriting, symbolizes his personality.

In the mountain he must choose his path between the crevasses ; the eye is often surer than the trail outlined.

At times Greloz and his companion stopped falling to fly, flung out by jagged places on the cliff.

They came to rest at last down on the glacier. They were bruised and bleeding, their clothes were in tatters but they had no serious injuries.

The mountain is sometimes capricious. It killed Emile Rey, called during his lifetime "The Prince of Guides", on a harmless ledge, but it spared Greloz, Valluet, and many others in spite of nightmarish falls.

You might think that after escaping miraculously from a long tête-à-tête with death those men would have given up the mountain. Not at all! The following Sunday, Greloz was already trying to climb the terrible north side of Dru, the wall seen from Montenvert.

Plainsmen are bewildered by this strange obstinacy.

★

THERE is a perpetual controversy between the climbers and the hikers.

For the first, the mountain doesn't exist below 1000 feet. For the others, "The Alps are at their most beautiful seen from below."

This was the opinion of the English essayist with the flowery pen, John Ruskin.

As a child he had discovered the mountain at Chamonix—there is a rock dedicated to him there—and until the end of his life—he died in 1900 in his 80's—he sang of it, painted it and even photographed it, for in 1849 he was one of the first to aim a camera at its splendors.

But he never climbed it.

"So as not to profane the work of God," he said. "Because that dear poet was a milquetoast, tyrannized by a domineering mother," whispered his enemies.

However that may be, he extolled the Alps and condemned the Alpinists. He accused them of turning the "Earth's Cathedrals" into "greasy poles."

Autumn makes a noman's land of the high ridges and peaks where deep winter reigns. In the valley, nature prepares for the worst by donning its gayest colors. This is the period when everything hangs in suspense, lies in wait. The chamois abandons the moraine for mountain pastures, the marmot burrows, the wood grouse makes the most of the last rays of sunshine. The guide takes possession of his farm again. The rifle replaces the ice-axe and the dog the roped party. Up there the refuges are locked up tight against the elements. On the Chardonnet ridge the traces of camping parties are wiped out, the holds are sealed by ice.
Nature has regained her equilibrium: on high, the great geological waiting period begins; below, life picks up where it left off.

His books were widely read and had unexpected results. After reading them, many Englishmen crossed the Channel and headed for the Alps, not to meditate in the shadow of those "Cathedrals" but to scramble right up them.

They even founded a club as exclusive as the Jockey Club. Before being admitted, one had to show his quarters of nobility; that is, several glorious ascensions. Its name was soon known the world over: the Alpine Club.

Who were its members? Young dare-devils? Hare-brains? Sons of wealthy families burning their candle as well as their father's fortune at both ends? Not at all! The list of members of the Alpine Club in 1863 proves it. Out of 281 members, 57 were barristers, 33 attorneys, 34 clergymen, 15 professors, and 19 belonged to the "gentry."

Level-headed people, as you can see, who went out for a new sport on what one of them called "the most beautiful playground in Europe."

In the middle of the 19th century most of the high mountains were still inviolate. Among them, the most famous perhaps after Mont-Blanc was Matterhorn, the pride of Zermatt.

Even today Zermatt has retained its originality. It is one of the rare cities of Europe which can only be reached by train. In the streets of its old quarter, among the toast-colored chalets of Valais, sports cars are replaced by horsedrawn, belled omnibuses.

It would seem that, following Ruskin's thoughts, the silence of God is being respected.

It stands alone.

It has tolerated no other peak near it. It resembles a sword blade pointing heavenward, a black blade with ice sparkling here and there, for on its sides no snow can cling. They are too steep. And the receding movement of its summit gives its proud grandeur the arrogance of a challenge.

But, like so many others, won't the Matterhorn

Is this a Genesis or an Apocalypse? The work of a demented town-planner? Who designed these boulevards and for what vehicles? The giant robot is hiding his hand. Like Zeno's arrow, it advances in its immobility.

This is the factory which manufactures the Rhone River. The glacier is as wide as the river, as if the latter were total, right from its origins. The personage on the center right, a forgotten peg, is a pebble during its thousand-year wait. Under it, scores of feet beneath, for the earth erodes ice better than the sky, a stream flows, a torrent soon to be set free to rush off to the sea.

The villages of Valais are built like a house: in stories. They are turned to the open spaces, hungry for light. Above this landscape of trees, vineyards and rich meadows, the snows of spring announce a land's-end.
Sometimes the eye can capture an austere stage setting, a passerby in his Sunday best, outlined on the strange dolmen which is an elevated barn. The hard granite is ever present: it conveys the personality of the rugged country encircling the hamlet.

Cursed by the Wandering Jew because its inhabitants refused him shelter, the rich region of Zermatt, where vineyards grew at the foot of a calm, sun-drenched peak, was surrendered to the devil's saraband.
Centuries later the old man without a country crossed over the Theodule Pass again. Through the blizzard he could momentarily perceive, at the foot of a monstrous skeleton of a mountain, a desert of ice and scree instead of the former smiling countryside. His heart sank. He let himself drop down onto a large rock and cried so long and hard that his tears formed a dark lake. And that is how, it is said around the hearths in the Saint Nicholas valley cottages, the Matterhorn came to be reflected in the Lac Noir.

be disappointing when we go around it? Admirable on this side, will it be a cow pasture mountain on the other? Not this time! Concessions are unknown to the Matterhorn. Seen from the Italian valleys it is as proud as ever and though it is no longer pyramidal, it resembles a crouching lion.

The poets of the nineteenth century were not sparing in the epithets they used to celebrate it. They compared it to a tower in ruin, to a rearing horse, to an obelisk wounding the sky, to a sphinx, to a torso. They named it the "Leviathan of Mountains," the "Achilles of the Alps."

Ruskin was shocked at first by its unusual form, then he became accustomed to it and proclaimed it "the most noble reef in Europe."

All these celebrants were in agreement on one point: *that* mountain would never be climbed. This was not the opinion of our English friends who decided to make Matterhorn a playground like the others.

And, shamelessly, they set out to attack its perils. They were twofold. To triumph over the Matterhorn, they had to affront both its precipices and its inns.

Occasionally, in the warmth of a hotel in Chamonix or behind the storm windows of a palace in Saint Moritz, we think back with nostalgia to those inns of the past, palaces of drafts and early morning racket.

But the Englishmen of Matterhorn, men of refinement, comfort-loving bourgeois, railed against them. Here is how one of them described his arrival at the Hotel du Mont Cervin at Valtournanche: "We were shown our beds in two corners of the same room which also served as the diningroom; one of the beds was only a sort of cupboard in the wall."

The innkeeper was a good sort but it didn't show on his face since, one night a traveler, terrified by his host, barricaded himself in his room with the aid of his alpenstocks.

1880 ALPINA 1955

It was forbidden to play Swiss pastoral melodies in the regiments from Valais or Vaud in the service of the king of France. Their famed bravery dissolved when they heard the songs of their country. Since then the Swiss have invented peace ; they can blow in horns to their hearts' content or parade, peaceful grenadiers, preceded by their canton's banner. Three faces: the descendant of Saint Bernard of Menthon and the guide from Zermatt flank the anonymous tourists who, from the top of Pilate, contemplate the Four Cantons Lake.
To each his insignia: the cane, the rope, the dog. To each his symbol: contemplation, fraternity, fidelity.

The prices, it must be admitted, were modest. A bed cost one franc and the food, that is four lunches, four dinners and two dozen eggs, eight francs.

And for that sum one was served "grissins" and "polente" and also a special dish, eggs *à la reine*, which amazed so many visitors that they wrote in a logbook now in our possession: "A masterpiece," and "An incomparable dish only to be found at Valtournanche."

In the middle of these appreciatory remarks is a more disillusioned comment written by a hiker just back from the Théobule Pass: "How can one climb so high and come back down so dumb!"

In this same book, on August 26, 1860, a client signed his name: Edward Whymper.

With him opens a new chapter in the history of the Alps.

Whymper, although born in the county of Suffolk, did not resemble the Englishmen who had preceded him. The Tyndalls and Stephens wore beards. Whymper was clean-shaven. He had already abandoned the frock-coat for more modern clothing.

Furthermore, he hadn't come to the Alps as a dilettante but for professional reasons. A London editor had commissioned this penniless artist to paint watercolors of Switzerland and Dauphiné.

On seeing the Matterhorn he had the same revelation as Ruskin but he wasn't a dreamer, even less a sportsman. He was a conqueror.

He liked mountains for the pleasure of being the first to the top of them—and he let no grass grow under his feet. He was the first to reach the top of Pelvoux, the Barre des Ecrins, the Aiguille d'Argentière, the Grandes Jorasses, the Aiguille Verte, the Mont Dolent. In a single 18-day campaign he climbed 100,000 feet of virgin mountain.

But they were mere trifles. What he really

Here is the Pyramid. It is neither that of Kephren nor a teocalli. Its blocks were never hauled by any slave.
"Everything is nourished by the sun, the wind and the moon," it was formerly written on an ancient port on the Aegean Sea. Born of stardust, of solid air and nocturnal tides, it is witness of what once was and of what will be.
But this Matterhorn, springing from dust and the original lavas, and such as we see it here, is the one discovered by Edward Whymper. He approached it as an archeologist would Pharaoh's tomb. He wanted to conquer it for the reason his compatriot did Mount Everest. The latter was asked, "Why climb to the top?" and he replied, "Because it's there."
On July 14, 1865, the peak was vanquished. On the way down four bodies were the tribute men had to pay to the great Pyramids.

wanted was that solitary peak which had already resisted his attacks on several occasions: the Matterhorn.

In July, 1865, Whymper decided to attempt the ascent by an Italian ridge. He asked Jean-Antoine Carrel, a guide from Breuil, to accompany him although he was an adversary as well as an ally. Carrel had already accompanied the Englishman on the Matterhorn but he had also tried to reach the top without him.

Carrel turned down his offer. He had accepted another invitation, he explained, that of taking a group of ladies for a hike. But what did Whymper learn the next morning? Carrel had lied to him. The "group of ladies" was none other than Giordano, the founder of the Italian Alpine Club, and the "hike" an expedition to the long-coveted summit. Furious, Whymper had only one idea in mind: beat the traitor to the top.

Giving up the plan of using the Italian ridge, he chose to climb the Hörnli ridge in Switzerland.

He improvised a caravan composed of two guides, Michel Croz of Chamonix—a master-guide—and Tangwalter from Zermatt, along with three other English gentlemen, the Reverend Hudson, Lord Douglas, and a nineteen-year-old named Hadow. Whymper did not know them and Hadow was only a novice but in order to have guides he had to allow them to bring their clients with them.

For the first time in his life, perhaps, that calculating man compromised. He was to pay for it for the rest of his life.

The ascent began, however, under the best conditions. There wasn't a cloud in the sky and the Hörnli ridge proved to be less steep than they had imagined.

On July 14, 1865, at 1: 40 p.m., the invincible Matterhorn was vanquished.

The party cheered but Whymper's joy was marred by a nagging worry. Where was Carrel?

Could Old Man Winter with his big, white, glacier-like beard and back bent over his gnarled stick which freezes, breaks, shatters, splits and pierces everything it touches, be the father of the Virgin which looks over Mürren?
The peasants wonder about this when on sunny days they listen to the rumbling of the avalanches on the pure and gloomy Jungfrau.

5.5
217
5.5
225
5.5
224

*T**he** Ouïbra used to fly over the Swiss lakes in olden times. But the shadow of the winged serpent, born of Pontius Pilate's uneasy soul, no longer floats over the gloomy slopes of the Quatre Cantons lake. From Geneva to Zurich, the sailboats care little about the breath of the legendary dragons. Perhaps a stronger evening wind blowing from Mount Pilate will push them into port.*

The lake is sometimes a gardener. In the midst of rocks and larches it is clever at lining up the rhododendrons and digitalis, placing the saxifrage, arranging the soldanella and gentians, concealing the adrosace and willowherbs, using all the dream flowers to create an Alpine garden.

He leaned over the chasm and saw the Italian guide and his clients climbing up the opposite side.

This sensible gentleman was seized by a fit of madness and began throwing stones at his unfortunate adversaries. Soon his companions began to imitate him, sending an avalanche of rocks down the mountainside.

The terrified Italians fled.

On the top, after fashioning a flag from a torn shirt to announce their victory to the valley below, the descent began.

Many Alpinists have noticed it. Accidents in the mountain most often occur without warning, at the moment when all danger seems past.

Whymper and his companions, roped together, walked slowly but unhesitatingly. The air was perfectly calm. Not a hint of wind. Not a cloud. All the mountain peaks were visible.

Of course, young Hadow was not at home on the steep rock but Michel Croz, one of the best guides of that period, was watching over him. They hoped to reach Zermatt before evening.

Suddenly, there was a cry. Hadow had stumbled, falling on Croz and knocking him down. Both men started sliding down the mountainside, dragging Hudson and Lord Douglas with them.

Whymper and Tangwalter set their backs against the cliff to try to break their fall—but to no avail. The rope broke between Lord Douglas and the Swiss guide.

The Matterhorn had taken four victims.

But that was not the end of it. To the horror of the accident was added a supernatural terror.

In the sky over the heads of the dazed men two big crosses took shape, transparent, colorless, silent like a vision from another world.

"A mirage," said Whymper to reassure his guide but Tangwalter wouldn't be convinced. The crosses' appearance right after the accident was a sign from heaven.

Whymper returned, dignified and silent, to

"A sonorous, vain and monotonous line." Vanity of the ever-dominated horizon; a church steeple ending in a pine tree; purity... There is a threshold of the imagination difficult to cross over between this white lowland and that burst of rock. The essence of the mountain? It is this chaos which repudiates the plain as the cliff flees the sea. The vertical is the distorted echo of the flat world.

The snow is white. Everything is white: the houses, the paper-wrapped package, the ski-jackets of the window-shoppers, the greens of this winter golf course which is called curling, the skating-rink and the airport, the sun silhouetted between the shadows on the bobsled which passes the wall of polar sound.
In the refuge, the glass of white wine.
This is Switzerland, as white as snow.

Zermatt and shut himself in his room at the Mont Rose Hotel. And there, once the door had closed behind him, he is said to have howled like a wounded wolf all night long.

After this tragedy he did not give up mountains since he went from the Andes to the Himalayas and to the Rockies but never again did he climb in the Alps.

The victims' graves were no sooner covered than tongues began to wag. It was whispered in cafés and on streetcorners that Tangwalter had cut the rope with his knife to save his own life.

He was called before his peers, the Company of Guides of Zermatt, who acquitted him. The decision did not give back his peace of mind for the decisions of justice are powerless against public suspicion and Tangwalter carried the burden of calumny to his death.

The tragedy at Zermatt soon became a sensational subject of conversation in Europe and the New World. Controversies and even polemics appeared in the newspapers. For lack of a photograph a terrible and fantastic drawing by Gustave Doré was published depicting the accident.

Ruskin was indignant. The greasy pole was no longer merely ridiculous. It was, hereafter, odious since murderous.

Queen Victoria herself was incensed. She thoroughly disapproved of such absurd sports which threatened to decimate the youth of her kingdom.

How difficult it is to talk to youth! One means to put them on guard against a peril and one only kindles their need for action. The royal remonstrances had but one effect: countless young men fled an England too Victorian for their taste.

In the Alps the relief troops for the reckless Englishmen were still more reckless Englishmen.

*

The true voyager travels in autumn. All alone he will sample the new wine while climbing slowly up to Saint Nicholas where the altitude still permits vineyards. The latter cling to slopes so steep that, according to the natives, even chickens need to be shoed like horses to hang on.

RECKLESSNESS didn't stop there. Some thought they found an explanation for that senseless craze for mortal risks in a valley of the Grisons.

"When Zarathustra was thirty years old, he left his home and the lake of his home and went into the mountains. There he enjoyed his spirit and his solitude, and for ten years did not weary of it," wrote Friedrich Nietzsche.

Zarathustra was Nietzsche himself. As for the mountain, refuge of the wise, it was Sils-Maria in Upper Engadine between Saint-Moritz and Maloja.

Imagine a Norway with the climate of Italy. Three lakes surrounded by a circle of high mountains: so much for Norway. But a stone's throw from the valley lies Chiavenna, Lombardy, another lake with a Mediterranean flavor, Lake Como.

With each hour of the day, with the color of the sky and the movement of the clouds, the landscape oscillates between those two poles: the sharpness of the Alps and the gaiety of the Riviera. Sometimes it passes without transition from the shadow of the sad larches to the turquoise of the lakes. At other moments the bright pastures are mirrored in an azure wave.

When Nietzsche discovered Engadine he wrote, "I seem to be in a Promised Land. A month of October full of calm and sun. For the first time I am finding relief."

Suffering from atrocious migraine headaches which made him half-blind, he had given up his teaching position in Bâle. He had believed in Germany and had been disappointed by the cumbersome, bureaucratic Germany under Bismarck. He had been Wagner's friend and companion of hard days.

One summer night in Bayreuth, Nietzsche placed on the musician's piano Brahm's "Triumphlied," superbly bound in red Morocco. Without a word, Wagner began to play the score. Suddenly, unable to contain his resentment, he exclaimed, "This is Mendelssohn bound in calf!"

It was, perhaps, before this landscape between Sils-Maria and Silvaplana that Nietzsche, during a lonely walk, first hit upon the reflections of Zarathustra and the theory of eternal recurrence.
He noted that this idea had come to him "6,000 feet above man and time... near Sils-Maria."
This took place in the month of August 1881: since then the snow has covered that fugitive summer eighty-two times with winters which Zarathustra called "sly guests sitting in my dwelling."

Was Archimedes right to declare: "Mountains are enormous stones thrown by infernal gods into the garden of the world because just and protective divinities can tolerate only plane surfaces…?"
On seeing the northern side of the Eiger we are tempted to believe him. Bodies, or shreds of bodies, still cling to it, forever conserved like mummies in a necropolis. Azure-colored or stormy, summer or winter, this peak belongs to an arctic universe. Desolate, dank, vertical, it is the storm's lover, a toboggan for the tempest and the avalanche, a trysting-place for the wind, hail, snow and lightning.
Its sister, the Jungfrau, is mischievous, too. It secretes fogs from which sulfuric fumes emerge. Its snows are deforming mirrors — the hole is only a hollow ; the plane surface an abyss.
In the bowels of these monsters a roller coaster has hewn a path: a rackrailway climbs and coils, dragging itself through a tunnel up to the Jungfrau desert.
A few black dots between Eiger and Jungfrau symbolize the tourists set down on a mound of hard, sure snow.

Nietzsche made no comment but later wrote these lines, "For me, henceforth, Wagner is no longer great."

Two years later the breach between the two was complete.

Friedrich Nietzsche, surrounded by the calm beauty of Engadine, was thus in a state of deep confusion. And yet that nearsighted, sickly, puny man with his walrus mustache was on the verge of one of the most stupefying adventures of the human mind.

Each year he returned to Sils-Maria to continue, in the calm of the mountains, his revolutionary work. He lived near the Fex bridge in a rustic chalet which still stands. Since he had a horror of noise, the owners gave him a small, low-ceilinged room with a single window opening on the mountain.

In this cell he worked day and often night. When he awoke at night the sound of his pacing up and down made the whole house shake. In the morning his hosts would beg him to get more sleep and let others do the same.

During his walks on the lakeshores or in the forests he would talk to the people of the valley. He was simple, pleasant, and modest but the strangeness of his eyes astonished people.

Children, however, enjoyed his company. He had the rare gift of knowing how to chat with them.

Last year in one of Sils-Maria's grocery stores, kingdom of humble treasures, two-for-a-penny candy, gilt-wrapped surprise packages, we met a very old woman who thought she had known him.

Her only comment was, "Lord! He was a strange one."

Of course he was strange. Wasn't a secret illness to plunge him a few years later into dementia praecox? But he could die to the world of Reason. He had said what he had to say.

He had written *The Will to Power*.

The water makes a detour to avoid the bouquet planted on a mossy rock. However powerful the waterfall it induces restful reverie. The Romantics knew this: in spite of the "Hideous Alps," the mountain is a haven of cascades and forests. From the black and white of the rocks and the rays of the sun, from the trees and the water is born an ethereal light, as mobile and changing as a human face.

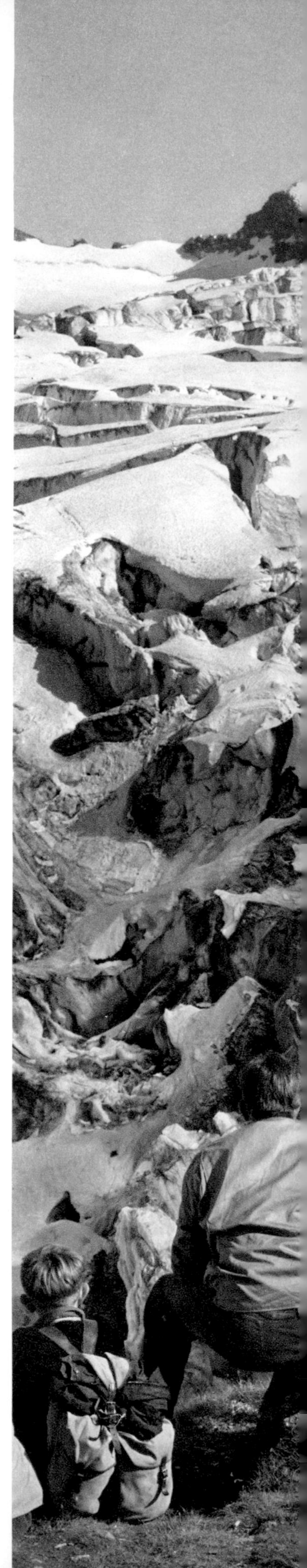

"Don't let children play with fire." These parents in the center are careless. The little boy on the right has already understood that a glacier is like the sky. Binoculars are needed to find one's way among all those starry shores. And from there it is simple to make the jump into the infinite…
… but the high-power telescope will make adults prudent: Move back to contemplate things from farther off.

"And Zarathustra went down among men, he announced to them that God was dead, he taught them the Superman."

★

ABOUT THAT TIME, Alpinism found its superman.

Eugen Guido Lammer, who was born in Vienna in 1862, would be a strange sight today if we were to meet him on a glacier. In his mountain climbs he always wore a hat and a romantic cape thrown back casually over one shoulder when the occasion permitted.

Tall, thin, and muscular, he was almost as near-sighted as Nietzsche. But Lammer was not to be stopped by such small details. He had an optician make him a pair of prescription-ground snow-goggles.

Under this rather ridiculous get-up was no ordinary man.

What was this rich bourgeois seeking in the Alps? He wrote, "I was possessed by an insatiable thirst for adventure and mortal danger, I was resolved to attempt the impossible and to lose no occasion to risk my life."

He climbed. "I was driven on by a current of demoniacal strength, I was a demon myself."

He fell, plunging down the mountainside. A fine occasion to test his self-control and, during the fall, to analyze every sensation. Sensations which, we are happy to say, were not at all disagreeable.

"I can tell you, my friends, it is a fine way to die!"

During his downward flight he was serene. "Not a trace of mortal fear nor moral anxiety." He remained foreign to himself, "a block of inert wood and my ego floating above the event like the spectator and the curious in a circus."

One small inconvenience: "The sun just opposite me, which through a swirling cloud of snow,

The last barns left behind, noman's land begins. The forest, like the labyrinth of séracs, is trackless. The pine trees are brought to an abrupt halt by the pure lined shadow of the very high perpendicular rock.

was so blinding that I had to close my eyes."

In his mind he saw his homeland, his mother, billiard balls bumping together. He thought of a friend: "Ha, ha! Now is when Professor Schulz would exclaim triumphantly, 'Yes, that is how it should end!'"

Thousands of other images cross his mind, but they are secondary to the cold and clear reckoning of the distance separating him from the bottom of the cliff; that is, from death. He thought of this death "passively, emotionlessly, without sadness, completely delivered from the chains of my ego."

Years, centuries seemed to pass during his fall, a fall of 700 feet.

"Then the roar of the cataract faded away, the whistling of the avalanche stopped. I opened my eyes and was filled with boundless amazement."

The mountain, as it would later be for Greloz and Velluet, had been merciful.

Lammer was not happy about it, quite the contrary. "No joy, no thanksgiving, no regret. But the wonderful passivity, the sweet nirvana had come to an end and already life's yoke had resettled on my shoulders: worries, plans, action; in brief, the famous unpleasant trinity."

In spite of serious injuries, he had to crawl to a refuge. Soon he could no longer crawl. He dragged himself and then he had no more strength to do even that.

He lay back on the moraine, looked up at the sky and thought of the words of Christ in agony: "Father, thy will be done!" He did not repeat these words but, as a disciple of Nietzsche, he cried out: "My will be done!"

He mustered up his last scrap of courage and began to crawl once more.

He reached the refuge. His "will to power" had saved him.

Such a man sets a dangerous example for he broke all the rules of safety. Not only did he scorn professional guides and their services but he was

The crumbling castles of the Dolomitic borderlands face the onslaught of clouds coming from Germanic glaciers. In this place, Italy has set up its ramparts against invasions from northern space. In spite of the battles waged against it by the demolished "Cinque Torri" ridges, the storm sometimes penetrates their line and swoops over the plain to rattle Venice.

The immemorial Adda glacier hollowed out the chasm which Lake Como fills up. The old moraines are peninsulas with villas whose names more readily evoke Tuscany or Venice than the peaks of Bernina or the Bergamask Alps. The church steeple is a vigilant sentinel turned towards the mountain to detect another of the glacier's advances into Latin country.

In the dale of Ampezzo the village of Cortina was not built by the "Maestri Comacini," those famous Lombard masons who emigrated to the Rhine and Danube regions. A city of chalets clusters around the church. In summer the tall slopes overlooking this refuge exude the scent of raspberry and huckleberry. In winter the snow descending from the Tondi di Falori or Mont Crépa opens the way to high adventure in skiing.

also one of the first to try very dangerous ascensions alone.

Once, however, he tolerated a companion. Even more surprising, a female companion, a lovely young woman named Paula.

It is true that the circumstances were exceptional. Lammer was on his honeymoon.

They had scarcely left the church before this metaphysical Alpinist was leading his bride, who had never set foot on a firn before, along an unbeaten trail.

The master and the debutante almost perished but on their return the valley people exclaimed, "She's worse than Lammer!."

Despite these feats Lammer's name would be forgotten—he had only conquered secondary peaks—if he had not written a book: *The Fountain of Youth.*

It was widely read and often misunderstood. It has often been used to justify rash acts.

Nietzsche's work, falsified by an unworthy sister, met with much the same misfortune. There again, in their doomed heredity, the two men bear a resemblance to each other.

★

ORDINARILY the tourist never comes in contact with the struggle on the mountain tops. He is sometimes shown, through the lenses of a telescope and for a modest sum, two black dots moving over a white surface, but it is impossible for him to reconstruct that abstract universe.

There is, however, a place in Switzerland, in the Oberland of Bern, where one can view high altitude Alpinism as from a theater box. It is Petite Scheidegg.

Behind the bay windows of its hotel looms the terrible northern face of the Eiger, an immense stage waiting for the actors of a spooky melodrama.

The theaters on the Boulevard of Crime had

There is a technique for climbing — and for photography too. One should not leap about in the mountains — except across crevasses. Rock requires a mastery which must not be confused with circus antics. With his shoulders, hands, feet, back, elbows, fingertips and even his nails, the rock climber must be one with the rock. He is a chimney sweep.

On the left we see the Italian Tyrol; on the right French Italy. The Ortiséi bulb-shaped bell-tower reminds us of Austria and the Central Alps. In the Aosta valley — one of Mont Blanc's seven valleys — the peasants after Mass speak French, their true provincial dialect. Strange Italy where, as during the Roman Empire, the frontier hesitates to burn its bridges between the Latins, eager to know the North, and the Celts and Teutons, ready to pounce on the sunny side.

their below-stages and trapdoors. The Eiger is true to that tradition. The inside of its flanks have been hollowed out to allow a mountain railway to reach Jungfraujoch by tunnel. An underground station even bears its name. Two windows have been opened right in the center, right where the height is the most impressive, where the wall is steepest, where the mountain's defenses are the most fearsome.

Nightmarish skylights which, we shall see, played a role in tragedy.

Two men from Munich attacked the Eiger by the north on August 22, 1935. Weather conditions were bad. Prudence forbade undertaking an ascension but the Germans scorned this virtue of weaklings. *They* belonged to the master race. Willpower was their middle name. They had been promised, in the event of victory, honors and roles in a film. The drizzle turned into a storm. The Eiger was blanketed in storm clouds.

When the wind died down, the mountain wall perceived through rents in the fog was like a sheet of ice. Yet, on this immense surface of ice a tiny human form was thought to be seen.

During the storm one of the two Germans must have fallen. His companion was still standing there on a ledge, silent, immobile.

He was dead. The frost had made a frozen statue of him.

A year later two Bavarians and two Austrians returned to the northern wall. They discovered the key passage for the ascension, a pass which was later given the name of one of those daredevils, the Hinterstoiser Pass.

They thought they had won. In reality, they had signed their own death warrants. Obliged to retreat, they could not cross the pass in the opposite direction. So there they stood, helpless, clinging to the mountainside which bad weather was again attacking.

Guides set out to assist them, passing through the railway skylights. After countless difficulties

From the resting platform (room for feet), invisible on the photograph, the climber has dealt with the following passages:
Fissure 5th degree (2 pitons).
Overhanging rock A2.
Sloping smooth rock A1.
Small straight passage (easy, good, shaky holds).
Dihedral angle of 5th superior.
The climber will now affront A2, a slightly overhanging ridge.
Above it, a slanting roof (3 firm pitons) defends the summit, not visible on the photograph. This is the Latin of high altitudes, the Greek of empty space, the declension of ascension ; in brief, the higher mathematics of dizzy heights. Mathematics or alphabet, algebra or plane geometry, always esoteric language, this is the key to the peaks.

they neared the place where the caravan in distress should have been. They shouted. A voice answered. Only one. The survivor screamed his name: Kurz, from Munich. His comrades were dead. One had fallen. One had frozen to death. The third was hanging in space at the end of a rope.

The Swiss guide could not reach Kurz and had to leave him, tied to two corpses. They returned the next morning and threw a rope to the Bavarian who was still alive after a horrible night. He even found the strength to slide down the rope.

Ten feet more and he would be saved. He struggled but couldn't budge. He was stuck.

They shouted advice and encouragement. For four long hours those men, separated by a few inches and five thousand feet of abyss below them, were to struggle.

One of the guides climbed on the shoulders of a comrade. With the end of his ice-axe he could touch the studs on Kurz's shoes.

Kurz muttered a few incoherent words. His arms dropped to his sides, his head fell forward, his whole body slackened. He appeared to be relaxed but in truth he had just died, died between heaven and earth at the very moment when he was perhaps about to be saved.

"We, the sons of the former Reich, united with our companions from the East, are hastening to victory!" the German, Heckmair thus announced, using the terminology in vogue at that time, the "first" on Eiger's north wall, a "first" which he accomplished on July 24, 1938, in the company of Voerg and the Viennese, Harrer and Kasparek.

What would poor Ruskin have had to say about this conquest? It was no longer enough to climb up the greasy pole, now it had been brought into the circus ring.

For three days reporters crowded against the windows in Petite Scheidegg, their noses pressed against the glass. One of them even rented a plane in order to fly over the climbing party.

Turning toward the East, the Julian Alps still shelter the royal eagle and the sparrow-hawk, the chamois and the grouse. On their pedestal of impenetrable forest they have the color of dolomite, that rose limestone which sunlight or storm changes to yellow or mauve. There, far from everything man can travel through the original Alps.

Black and white, the Altitude's ship is reflected on the Zell am See. It follows the course of the sun and shadow. The main masts are anchored: the captain woodcutter alone can rig them up. They were planted centuries ago, born of the first great Quaternary trees, springing from the first seeds germinated under a young sun. Nothing is more restful than to sit facing the panorama of the lakes and to guess what breeze or what light has just skimmed over their surface to animate the vegetal shadows and the immobile universe of the mountain.

Two bivouacs, a storm, a few injuries, cases of frostbite and falls furnished articles and justified his expenses.

After the victory our four climbers devoured six veal chops apiece and returned to Great Germany to let Hitler crown them with laurels.

They, too, were to perish, victims of that Mountain of man's overweening pride.

★

SOME EVENINGS in the South Seas, at the instant when the sun sinks on the horizon, there may be seen a strange light. This is the famous "green ray" which one of Jules Verne's heroes pursued in vain.

That lover of optical sensations seemed unaware of a phenomenon just as curious and to be found much closer to his native France, the "red ray" which is seen in the Alps and, more especially, in Italy in the Dolomites.

But, after all, aren't the Dolomites the land of the extraordinary? Don't they succeed in astounding even those who have just seen all the Alps most important marvels? And they do so without any spectacular glaciers—or almost.

Geologists describe the Dolomites, which owe their name to a French mineralogist, Déodat Gratet of Dolomieu, as a mixture of carbonate of lime and carbonate of magnesia having a widely varying resistance to erosion. This explains the towers, jagged peaks, and vertical cliffs.

A poet who visited them would probably think of Dante. Imagine, placed on pedestals of scree, gigantic columns bathed in the whole gamut of red, from pale pink to crimson. Titanic columns, pillars to hold up the heavens, it has been said.

The Dolomites' history is in no way inferior to their geography. Along these walls man has surpassed the limits of his daring, vanquishing that which is worse than the vertical—the overhanging.

Winter has congealed the stage setting. Nothing has been left out of this model of an Arlberg village: neither bulbular towered church facing East, nor hotels, nor actors. The funicular car is suspended between two pines. Like a skier on his mark, the countryside hesitates a moment before coming to life.

So danced the gnomes on the peaks of crystal and amethyst which covered the young Alps. They must have taught their dances to the first inhabitants of Tyrol. Rather than mock battles the "hand to hand" demonstrations resemble some sort of gigantic recreation: slap on the hand, tap on the cheek, slap on the thigh. One must be exhausted before dropping onto a rustic bench to joke with the girls while awaiting a pitcher of beer or white wine.

These mountains, it is true, lend themselves to exceptional feats for there is no snow. They can be climbed in rope-soled shoes. No difficult return to fear either for more often than not those vertical walls hide a much more good-natured back which can be rapidly descended with hands in pockets.

The Dolomites are also battlefields. During the First World War, the Italians and Austrians fought furiously here.

One skirmish has remained famous. One night a certain Sepp Innerkopler, holder of the Austrian Gold Medal, climbed the northern wall of the Cima Picola, one of the most difficult sides of the mountain, in order to range the artillery. He was still climbing when a member of the Italian ski troops, De Luca, surprised him. An epic struggle ensued in the darkness of the edge of the precipice. Innerkopler was defeated and fell into space.

Luiz Trenker has recounted this war, in which troops went to the front in improvised ski lifts, in his film "The Flaming Mount."

As the second storm blew up in 1939, the same bellicose spirit reigned in the Dolomites. From Munich came climbers stirred up by propaganda and ready for any sacrifice. One of them had exclaimed, "We Germans have nothing more to lose."

The Italians, stung to the quick, vied with them in daring.

Over the grave of a casualty these words were spoken, "A climber has fallen. May one hundred others come forward to avenge him."

Exalted youth today no longer want to be satisfied with their own muscles. To triumph over gravity they drive pitons into the rock, they use snaplinks, they have themselves hoisted by rope to get by several yards of overhanging rock.

After free climbing, it invented artificial climbing and "directissima," that is, climbing which

Men and their houses, gods and their churches. The villa and the sanctuary are only refuges. The soul of the landscape overpowers man's effort: upward, toward the pines, toward the glacier, toward the scarcely visible rocks...
The sky is higher than the steeple.

must follow a plumb line from the pebbly foot right up to the top.

A native of Munich had the idea of classifying the difficulties. Henceforth, one will speak in terms of a passage of the "sixth inferior degree," that is, "very difficult," or of the "sixth superior degree" or "at the limit of human endeavor."

The Italians went even further. In the Dolomites and beyond the Dolomites the great Alpine surfaces had been vanquished so they thought up the spiral ascent. They climbed the Matterhorn passing over all four sides.

They were decorated for this preposterous exploit.

★

LET'S COME back down to the less heroic Alps, the Alps in winter.

For a long time the snow stopped the chalet clocks. Half-buried villages still lived in the nineteenth century. This backwardness had its charm.

While skiing around a high, deserted mountain and devouring the frozen eggs of a winter picnic, one could pretend to be living the high adventure of Mr. Whymper's day.

In soundly sleeping hamlets, strange things could be seen such as clients around a pot-bellied stove playing "Beast" with cards, beans, nuts and logs.

Then a revolution broke out in an Austrian valley at the end of which skiing, a mountain game, had become a sport for city-dwellers.

That put on end to winter solitude.

Without going back to prehistoric times, Norway and Sweden were the two cradles of skiing and it was only around 1873 that those long wooden slats appeared in the Alps.

Sir Arthur Conan Doyle, father of Sherlock Holmes, was one of the first to put on the contraptions.

Judging from the following article, the technique was still rudimentary: "Skiers let their skis lead them at will until the air acts as a natural brake and brings them to a stop." Or this one:

Mountaineers in Lilliput?
The chasms are playing hide-and-seek so that this side of the Kalkögel looks like a rock at Fontainebleau.
The mirage could only deceive a contemplative spectator. The mountain climbing school teaches on an Alpine scale. The equation, from base to summit, is resolved in hours and yards of cord.

Salzburg and Innsbruck. These two cities are the Austria of the Alps for Vienna is elsewhere. Music and skiing, like the light of springtime and the snow, play a game of the seasons. Festival and sports. At Innsbruck winter has frozen the scenery. At Salzburg the bells of Residentplatz are going to fly off to Rome or fall into the fountain where Triton and Atlas are reining in their horses.

"In a descent, the skier leans on his pole and closes his eyes. Then he descends, straight as an arrow, until he can no longer breathe. He then throws himself sideways in the snow."

The Scandinavians had delivered the skis but no instructions for how to come to a stop. It was necessary to re-invent the "Christiana" and the "Telemark," that graceful genuflection which permits skiers to trace a quarter circle on the snow.

These two stops were the keys to skiing until the day when a native of the Austrian valley of Arlberg had an inspiration. He started out on a crusade against the Telemark, that system of stopping which went against the laws of Nature.

In truth, the Telemark and its genuflection were not suitable for Arlberg's steep slopes.

Much ink was spilled on the snow but Schneider, the apostle, won out. The Telemark had to relinquish its place to the "stembogen," born of the old "snow-plow." The School of Arlberg made the valley a terribly fashionable place.

For once, let's not criticize fashion. Arlberg deserved its consecration.

Its sites are charming without being affected. There, the solemn rubs shoulders with the pastoral, the pass hewn out of the rock usually leads to a meadow or to a natural lake or one created by human hands.

Furthermore, the country has touristic references. Noah is said to have run his ark aground here at the end of the Deluge and, in the joy of being on firm land again, fathered the ancestors of all the good people of Arlberg today.

Fortified by such illustrious stock, they have a tendency to irreverence and the Austrian Emperor Joseph II called them the "Impossibles." You won't suffer from this character trait for, however insolent they may be to Power, they are extremely pleasant to visitors and the most considerate hosts in all Europe.

But let's return to Schneider and his new technique. That pioneer was not content to replace

Avalanche or fog? The forest is on fire. Gustave Doré might have painted this cataclysm as an illustration for the Divine Comedy. *It is Vulcan's den; it is the Acheron's final leap.*

In Kitzbühel golden wedding anniversaries are celebrated on Sunday. Madame sports an outstanding hat and Monsieur a remarkable pipe. Or perhaps one dresses up every Sunday for the sheer pleasure of feeling young again. In Zillertal widows return home from Mass, their eyes to the ground. God must have given them a fear of heights for in the low valleys of the Tyrol or Styria, the mountain is "for the cows."
In Shoms, children ring door bells. Visit or prank? In ten years they will be puffing away at a cold pipe.
Kitzbühel, Zillertal, Shoms... Austria likes hats, decorated belts, leather pants, heavy pipes — but here folk costumes are not disguises.

a gliding stop by a skidding one. He gave to skiing what it had lacked until then: a creed.

Before 1930, one learned to ski in a completely hit and miss manner, at the risk of falls and sprains. Schneider created classes with schedules, examinations, prizes for excellence and certificates of merit.

It was a brainstorm for in the heart of every man lingers a nostalgia for the classroom. There was a rush on Arlberg where each was treated as a dunce or promising according to his capabilities.

Of course, the school soon had competition. It was dethroned by the French method but this was really only due to transfers of instructors. Skiing was in vogue and it soon evolved from pedagogical to universal.

Better still, it became a vital necessity. We go off to winter sports today as naturally as we eat and sleep. To deprive ourselves of it would be to perish.

★

LET'S CROSS a frontier. There's no need to hesitate for we'll feel as much at home in the Bavarian Alps as in the Austrian.

Their sign is the Lion, the Bavarian Lion, heraldic animal of the Wittelsbach dynasty which reigned for seven centuries. This wild beast with his well-groomed mane is found everywhere, in the stone of the churches and on the café signs.

The best way to visit this beautiful region whose only factories are old forges on the edge of the torrents and whose chief wealth are the forests and pastures covering two-thirds of its surface, is to go on foot and in short pants like the natives.

This means of locomotion will permit you to become acquainted with inn-life, and the inns in these Alps are charming. The food may seem a bit heavy but the gaiety is so natural that you will quickly forget the richness of the sausages and cabbage.

You'll join in the singing and you'll try to

On the crest live only lichen and moss, the flora of an oxygen-scarce world where sunbeams can be fatal. From the glacier, where the only life is the short agony of lost butterflies, flows the hard, dust-laden water down to the lake which, as Michelet declared, transforms wild water into living water. Above the tallest rock the sky dominates, itself a fathomless lake. And the forest plunges, as if in search of its origins, into the deep water of the lake, so deep that it comes toward us, brimming over as if toward another infinity.

yodel. If you are not successful you can console yourself by thinking that the Carusoes of the yodel must be a trifle goitrous.

The next day you'll set off again and at each turn in the road you'll discover the picturesqueness of the region. Houses with a single tiled wall, the west one from which bad weather comes. Brightly painted façades like doll's faces. Baroque churches and bulb-shaped bell towers. The Allgau, the milk country. The Höll Ravine and its leaping waters. Oberammergau and its Passion Play which has been enacted once in every decade since the great plague of 1633.

Keep your eyes and ears open, for the picturesqueness of this country is not confined to reality, it is also present in the world of fancy. You'll hear tell of a mountain grotto which withstands the fury of a still living, imprisoned Charlemagne. On the steep-sloped Lake Königsee, the boatman will blow his bugle to awaken an echo. You will be shown a petrified king on top of a ridge. He was a bad prince. And if you pass by Oberberoberg on January 1st you'll hear the cannons chasing the Old Year out.

Sometimes, in the midst of this riot of local color, before these gorges seemingly designed by Dürer and these lakes worthy of a symphony by Richard Strauss, one wonders if all this hasn't been arranged by a chamber of commerce on a colossal scale. The Germans are such organized people.

No, the Neuschwanstein castle is entirely authentic in its disproportion.

Its builder was King Louis II of Bavaria who reigned from 1866 to 1886. This monarch was a choice subject for literary men who made of him a Hamlet whose Elsinore was perched on a Bavarian peak, who baptised him the mad king, the virgin king, the misanthropic prince. Gabriel d'Annunzio wrote: "Louis of Bavaria is truly a king but a king of himself and of his dream."

"King of himself..." A beautiful description of

The great schuss of Arlberg! Turns... the pure lines of the descent... speed... reveries...
In these mountains, the most secret, the most hidden of the Alps, Alpine skiing was born; a sport for mountaineers, for men climbing slowly to the rhythm of slipping seal skins, a sport for explorers. The skier's white universe is tinted blue by the shadows. It is cold. The sun is hard at work sharpening the peaks, designing beaches of light, sculpturing the asymmetry of the slopes. It is time for the black dots which are men to return to the valley.

The meditation of the happy few.

Parading caterpillars or the underground activity of moles? A strange gray procession crawls around the white church. The sun must be stingy with its rays in this valley for hay, like a washing, to be hung out to dry.

the solitary sovereign to whom Verlaine dedicated an enthusiastic sonnet beginning with these lines:

"King, only true king of this century, hail, Sire.
You wanted to die avenging your reason
On things political, on folly,
On that Science intruding in the house."

That melancholy prince who feared men and fled from women had one passion: castles. He ruined himself building castles. He compromised his reign, he lost his crown for the sole pleasure of building his beloved castles. He also had one love: Wagner, whom he helped and led to fame. These two passions sometimes merged since Neuschwanstein—the new land of the swan, Lohengrin's swan—is dedicated to the author of the Tetralogy and his music.

Before building Neuschwanstein, a medieval burg erected in the second half of the nineteenth century, Louis did research but not, as one might expect, in the precious and archaic archives to which his rank gave him access, but by visiting the 1867 exposition to which Napoleon III had invited him and by admiring the feudal dwellings there in pasteboard.

Plans were submitted to him. To the great dismay of his advisors, one project aroused his immediate enthusiasm. It was not signed by an architect but by the decorator of the Royal Opera House.

The theater man was chosen. He could well be proud for never had such a production been entrusted to one of his colleagues. The setting? One of the most romantic gorges in the Alps. Dark forests descend the ravines which disappear into chasms on the bottom of which sparkles the wild foam of the torrents.

The castle? It was raised on a peak of unstable rocks. "The king of his dreams" didn't care. A despot when his own caprices were in question, he ordered that they be reinforced with many walls and pillars.

On this scaffolding the decorator piled up

The "great bellringer" who watched over Tyrol and Corinthia had been sleeping for hundreds of centuries. He was awakened by a priest.
Count Franz Altgraf von Salm, bishop of Gurk, curious about what went on in the silence of the tall mountains, issued a cordial invitation to eleven clergymen, nobles and scholars all, to go with him to the highest of Glockner's peaks. On July 28, 1800, *assisted by* 19 *guides, the group reached the top.*
Today cars can reach the glacier's wide boulevard. But as soon as the road is left behind the man of the mountain finds silence and solitude again. Occasionally, after a blast of wind, an indistinct sound is heard on the distant Grossglockner.

Zimmer
A. Jocher
Ansichts-
karten
Frankfurter Allgemeine
Tabak-
waren
Lorenz Maier

In summer Upper Bavaria lives at a slower pace, at the rhythm of the artisans and shops. The Dolomitic peaks are silhouetted against the sky, circus and playground for climbers from Munich. On the house a sky is painted; one can even rent a room on the bishop's side or on the monk's. But in the evening when the shutters close on the glory of heaven and on the stars, one can sacrifice a little sleep to the accordion, smoke and beer.

machicolations, watch-towers, battlements, overhanging turrets, pointed roofs. It was a veritable repertory for a student of the Beaux Arts.

In this palace worthy of a tale by Hoffmann, Louis lived alone with an aide-de-camp. At night, preceded by a torchbearing lackey, he would wander through all the useless splendor, passing from the baroque salons to the Music Room. He would gaze at the frescoes depicting the life of Parsifal or Wagnerian symbols carved along the staircases: the arms of King Artus, the cup of the Holy Grail, the Holy Dove. He would sit on an ivory throne in the center of an unfinished basilica.

★

LOUIS OF BAVARIA died at the bottom of a lake, assassinated by his dementia but even today visitors to Neuschwanstein and its hideous magnificence sometimes dream as Louis used to dream.

They think back with nostalgia to the Alps of yesteryear, today cluttered with funiculars, ski-lifts, ski-tows, train or automobile tunnels.

Those people possibly love the Alps' past but they don't love the Alps themselves.

They are unaware of the destiny of these mountains. Since the Romantic Age, the Alps have become the backbone of Europe. There is not a jolt in the modern world that does not make their fibers quiver. All the turns of the mind and the crises of contemporary politics were born or had an echo in their valleys. Rousseau and the Encyclopedists discovered Nature here. Nietzsche wrote his *The Will to Power* here. Louis of Bavaria, the sleepwalking king, dreamed his reign here. The last war only grazed them but it was from the heights of Berchtesgaden that Hitler led his armies to disaster.

How could the Alps have remained out of that great revolution of our time, the technical revolution?

The Alps—and therein lies their greatness—

At the flowery sign of the Virgin and Child, of the Huntsman and Stag, the inn welcomes you. Hunting is difficult near Nebelhorn and in the Kaiser-Gebirge mountains but tonight at dinner the leg of venison with currants or the stuffed grouse will astonish and delight the tourists far more tired than the hunter.

GASTHOF

are not a museum. They cannot be visited stretched out in a gondola.

They insist on being hiked in, climbed, scaled, their cliffs hewn, attacked with pitons, vanquished and subdued while, below, others are digging, excavating, raising, building, flooding. The Alps are a place of action. "The most beautiful playground in Europe," and also the biggest workshop for the most daring enterprises.

And for lovers of "idle hours" the Alps are vast. With a little searching, they'll find a forgotten village where "Beast" is still played and where a travelling companion will say, roughly, "Keep going!"

What is architecture? An upward effort toward the sky? The admirable church of Saint Bartholomew on the shore of the Königssee is worthy of a city. Here, it is crushed and diminished. Even if it were a cathedral its spires would be nothing in comparison with the perfect architecture of the planet.

The fate of all men was decided in and above this romantic countryside but the Berchtesgaden haunt is a deserted eagle's nest.
Boat or sleigh, tourist or peasant in Sunday dress, winter or summer, nature and life pass over History.
Will two happy children be the promise of a world at last at peace?

THE GREAT HOURS IN THE ALPS' HISTORY

Compiled by MAX ALDEBERT

50 to 30 million years (?) B.C.

Birth of the Alps.

circa 15000 (?) B.C.

First traces in the pre-Alps of Salève and Vuache on the edge of ancient glaciers, of Magdalenian hunters.

circa 3000 B.C.

Infiltration of the civilization of *palafitta* (prehistoric dwellings on stilts) in the Alps and installation of Neolithic tribes on the Swiss lake shores.

circa 1600 B.C.

The Ligures of the Third Bronze Age inhabit in part what they undoubtedly called the "Alp".

circa 500 B.C.

Tène era: the Iron Age in the Alps, especially on the banks of the Neuchâtel lake.

circa 300 B.C.

The Allobroges settle in Savoy, the Norics and the Phaetians in Austria.

218 B.C.

Hannibal crosses the Alps, probably at Mont Genèvre.

Ist Century

First Roman transalpine roads: legend has it that the one from Aoste to Vienna in Gaul was traveled by Pilate on his return from Galilea.

982

Bernard of Menthon founds the Grand Saint-Bernard convent on "Mont Jovis" (8,110 ft.).

1336

Ascension of Ventoux (6,273 ft.) by Petrarch who wrote an account of it.

1358

Ascension of Rochemelon (11,604 ft.) by Bonifacio Rotario, a fisherman wishing to "save his soul."

1492

On the order of Charles VIII, his chamberlain, Antoine de Ville and "his men" climb Mont Aiguille in Dauphiné (6,879 ft.).

1511

Leonardo da Vinci reaches a certain "Monboso", undoubtedly Monte Bô (8,386 ft.) opposite Mont Rose. First description of the art of climbing and painting mountains.

1580

Montaigne crosses the Brenner and Mont Cenis passes.

1603

Saint Francis of Sales, in a letter, uses in place of "Mons Maudite" the term "Mont Blanc". First known use of the latter.

1741

"Expedition" of the English Windham and Pocock to the "ice houses of Chamouni". They go up to the Sea of Ice (6,233 ft.).

1760

Horace Benedict de Saussure promises a reward to anyone reaching the summit of Mont Blanc. First attempt by Pierre Simon of Chamonix.

1775

The "wall" of 13,000 feet is crossed: A camping group reaches the Grand Plateau of Mont Blanc.

1779

An Englishman, Blair, finances the construction of a hut on Montenvers (6,233 ft.), first attempt at a refuge. Goethe will spend a night there.

1784

Marc-Théodore Bourrit's guides reach the Dôme du Goûter (14,120 ft.), two hours from the top of Mont Blanc.

1786

First ascension of Mont Blanc (15,781 ft.) by Jacques Balmat and Doctor Paccard.

1787

Second ascension of Mont Blanc by Saussure and his 18 guides. First scientific observations in high altitudes.

1790

Saussure draws up a plan for building a "wagon road" under Mont Blanc. His tunnel will be completed in... 1964!

End of XVIII th Century

Construction of transalpine carriage roads on the Brenner, Tende, Mont Cenis, Mont Genèvre and Simplon passes.

1800

Bonaparte passes the Grand Saint-Bernard. Stendhal follows the army. Von Salm, bishop of Gurk, with "eleven Alpinists" and nineteen guides, climbs to the top of Grossglockner (12,460 ft.).

1804

On the order of the Archduke John of Austria, Doctor Gebhart and two guides reach Ortler (12,792 ft.), summit of Austria.

1808

First feminine ascension: the Chamonix servant, Marie Paradis, to the top of Mont Blanc.

1812

First ascension of the Jungfrau (13,642 ft.).

1813

The Baron of Rambuteau, prefect of Simplon, pursued by the Austrian army, leads his civil servants over the Forclaz Pass (4,987 ft.) in the dead of winter.

1816

Shelley stays at Chamonix.

1820

First accident "officially registered" in mountain climbing: death by avalanche of three of Doctor Hamel's guides on Mont Blanc.

1821

Foundation of the first "Company of Guides" at Chamonix.

1828

Ascension of Pelvoux (12,946 ft.).

1834

Victor Hugo crosses the Sea of Ice in the company of the guide, Michel Devouassoud.

1838

George Sand and Liszt at Chamonix. The canoness, Henriette d'Angeville, jealous of George Sand's literary glory, reaches the top of Mont Blanc. First climbing exploit of the upper class.

1842

J.D. Forbes inaugurates the "high altitude promenade": from Chamonix to Zermatt by the glaciers.

1844

John Ruskin climbs Buet (9,977 ft.).

1851

Albert Smith, first "public relations man", goes to Mont Blanc and comes back with lectures.

1852

Establishment of first mountain hotel at Zermatt.

1853

Foundation of first high altitude refuge. The Grands Mulets on Mont Blanc (10,010 ft.).

1854

First ascension without guide: Steinberger on Koenigspitze.

1855

Ascension of Mont Rose (15,216 ft.).

1856

Count Fernand de Bouillé floats the white fleur-de-lis flag on top of the Aiguille du Midi (12,605 ft.). First political ascension.

1857

Foundation in London of the first Alpinist club: the *Alpine Club.*

1857–1870

Drilling of the Mont Cenis tunnel. Beginning of transalpine railways.

1860

Visit of Napoleon III and the Empress to Montenvers.

circa 1860

The ice hatchet is replaced by the piolet.

1860–1865

Conquest of the great peaks: Ecrins, Mont Dolent, Dent Blanche, Weisshorn, Grandes Jorasses, Aiguille Verte, Wetterhorn, Piz Bernina, Mönch, Lyskamm, etc.

1865

Pivotal year in the history of Alpinism. End of "heroic times" and beginning of modern Alpinism:
— Edward Whymper conquers Matterhorn (14,780 ft.) on July 14. During the descent four of his companions perish: Michel Croz, Hadow, Hudson and Lord Douglas. A few days later the Italian team composed of Carrel and Goret reaches the top.
— beginning of acrobatic climbing in the Aiguilles of Chamonix.
— an English team reaches the top of Mont Blanc by the very difficult Brenva way.
— first trial of a rack railway in Switzerland by Riggenbach (the Riggi railway was built from 1868 to 1875).

1869

Construction at Lancey of the first high pressure main supplying a turbine.

1870

First scaling of pure rock in the Dolomites.

1877

First ascension of Meije (13,067 ft.) by Boileau de Castelneau and Gaspard and son.

1880–1914

Innumerable "firsts" by Mummery (Grépon, Grands Charmoz, Dent du Requin, etc.) and by Fynn, Gugliermina, Pfann, Zsigmondy, Purtcheller, Young, Rian, Mayer, Fontaine, Lochmatter, Knubel, Carrel, Dibona, Ravanel le Rouge, etc.

1882

Queen Victoria asks Gladstone to prevent Englishmen from going off to the Alps and killing themselves. The Prime Minister finds no legal method of stopping them.

1889

Monsignor Achille Ratti camps on the top of Mont Rose and achieves the first crossing of the Zumstein Pass. In 1922 he will become Pope Pius XI.

1890

Construction of the observatory and refuge at Vallot (14,311 ft.). Skiing is introduced in Germany and Switzerland by the Norwegians.

1893

On Eiffel's plan, construction of the ephemeral Janssen refuge on top of Mont Blanc.

1904

First ascension on skis of Mont Blanc by Hylins.

1907

First ski contest on Mont Genèvre.

1909–1914

Construction of glacier funicular (7,887 ft.) at Chamonix.

1914

Parmelin, from Geneva, flies over Mont Blanc for the first time.

1914–1918

High altitude combats in the Dolomites between Austrians and Italians.

1919–1925

With the foundation of the High Mountain Group, Alpinism without guides triumphs.

1921

First plane lands in the high mountains: Durafour on the Dôme Pass (13,124 ft.) in a biplane, "Caudron".

1922

Creation of the *Gran Paradiso* National Park. First area for the protection of the Alpine flora and fauna.

1924

First winter Olympic Games at Chamonix. Development of winter sports stations in the Arlberg and Tyrol valleys.

1925–1939

German, French and Italian Alpinists resolve the last big Alpine problems: the northern walls (Mont Blanc, 1928; Aiguilles du Diable, 1928; Droites, 1930; Matterhorn, 1931; Grandes Jorasses, 1935; Drus, 1935; Ailefroide, 1936; Eiger, 1938; Eperon Walker, 1938; etc.). Classification of mountain climbing in degrees of difficulty. Beginning of artificial climbing.

1926

Ascension of Meije in April by A. Delille and P. Dalloz: first "winter" climb.

1942

First long high altitude film: "Premier de Cordée".

1945

The highest battle in the world on Géant Pass at almost 13,200 feet, between the Germans and French.

1945–1962

Triumph of artificial climbing. The northern walls become classics. Guides are recruited among the amateurs. The great climbs at the limit of the possible (Cima Grande di Lavaredo, Grand Capucin, Noire de Peuterey, Mont Blanc itineraries...) are popular. One man symbolizes the superhuman limits of mountain climbing: the Italian guide, Walter Bonatti (six bivouacs, alone, to climb the southwest pillar of Dru).

1952

The "Malabar Princess", long-distance mail plane, crashes on the summit of Mont Blanc.

1955

Construction of funicular on the Aiguille du Midi (12,605 ft.) which, stretching over the Vallée Blanche, permits a "bird's-eye view" of the Mont Blanc mountain mass.

1956

The death of Vincendon and Henry sets off a newspaper campaign against the "Homicidal Alps" (sic).

1960

First winter ascension of the Eiger's northern wall, reputed to be one of the most difficult even in summer.

1962

The French and Italian miners come together, opening the Mont Blanc tunnel.

ALL THE PHOTOGRAPHS ILLUSTRATING THIS WORK ARE BY **MICHAEL SERRAILLIER**, except **MACHATSCHEK**, p. 13 (in color), THE MEIJE AND THE GRAVE; p. 55, THE RHONE GLACIER; p. 65, THE JUNGFRAU; - **ROGER PERRIN**, p. 21, A CORDED PARTY ON TACUL; p. 36, DESCENT ON A DOUBLED ROPE IN CREVASSE; - **J. J. LANGUEPIN**, p. 38, ON THE NANTILLAIS PASS; - **JANINE NIEPCE**, p. 37, ASCENSION IN THE CHAMONIX VALLEY; - **JEAN IMBERT**, p. 73, (in color), THE VALLEY IN AUTUMN; - **Office National Suisse de Tourisme (Photo by ERWIG A. SAUTTER)**, p. 71, THE SKATING RINK OF MÜRREN; - **E. N. I. T.**, p. 90, THE VALLEY OF GARDENA IN THE DOLOMITES; p. 91, ANTAGNOT IN THE VALLEY OF AOSTE; - **Office du Tourisme Yougoslave**, p. 95, THE MARTULJK MOUNTAIN CHAIN IN THE JULIAN ALPS; - **Office National Autrichien du Tourisme (Photo by NUSSBAUMER)**, p. 107, INNSBRUCK IN WINTER; **(Photo by SROSSAUER)**, p. 115, SKIING IN ARLBERG; - **Office du Tourisme Allemand**, p. 125, THE SAINT BARTHOLOMEW CHAPEL ON THE KÖNIGSEE; p. 126, SLEIGHING PARTY AT MITTENWALD; **(Photo MÜLLER-BRUNKE)**, p. 126, IN THE BERCHTESGADEN REGION; **(Photo ERNST BAUMANN)**, p. 127, BOAT ON THE KÖNIGSEE.

PRINTED IN FRANCE THE 15th OF NOVEMBER 1962
FOR EDITIONS SUN IN PARIS, THE BLACK AND
WHITE ILLUSTRATIONS WERE PRINTED BY BRAUN
IN MULHOUSE AND THE ILLUSTRATIONS IN COLOR
BY DRAEGER IN PARIS.

4